National
History

Mary McLeod
BETHUNE
in
WASHINGTON, D.C.

Mary McLeod
BETHUNE
in
WASHINGTON, D.C.

Activism & Education in Logan Circle

Dr. Ida E. Jones

Charleston · London

THE
History
PRESS

Published by The History Press
Charleston, SC 29403
www.historypress.net

Front cover: Mary McLeod Bethune, by Paul Lanquist (paul@paullanquist.com), 2009. *Courtesy of the National Park Service.*
Back cover, lower: Mary McLeod Bethune and Mrs. William Hastie are seen protesting on Fourteen and U Streets, Northwest. *Courtesy Moorland Spingarn Research Center, Prints and Photographs Division.*
Back cover, upper: Mrs. Bethune, Dorothy Ferebee and four others are pictured at the dedication of the council house. *Courtesy Mary McLeod Bethune Council House, NPS.*

First published 2013

Manufactured in the United States

ISBN 978.1.62619.006.1

Library of Congress CIP data applied for.

Contents

Foreword

Once in a century, a person comes along who will change the way everyone views the world while simultaneously fueling worldwide social movements. Passionately committed to all methods of social reform, Mary McLeod Bethune created institutions that improved the daily lives of people on the local, regional, national and international levels. This study seamless fuses together the life of Mary McLeod Bethune while creating a new base for appreciating the life of a remarkable activist and agent of change.

My interest in the National Council of Negro Women's (NCNW) and Mrs. Bethune's role in community-based activities was tremendously stimulated when I spoke to longtime residents of the community where she lived in the nation's capital. As I listened to the words of people like Mrs. Amy Bundy, Mrs. Mary Sprow and Mrs. Jessie Carter, I learned of her support for the block clubs. The written and photographic materials accumulated from the early 1920s by Mrs. Eliza Johnson provide clear evidence of the many ways this national figure encouraged local women's garden clubs. I read through documents from activities at local churches and the community YWCA to learn the myriad ways this major figure in history created a remarkable legacy in her District of Columbia community. Dr. Jones's research illuminates my research on numerous levels.

In this book, Dr. Ida E. Jones uses multiple approaches for inquiry by focusing on Dr. Bethune's organizational advancement, government program development and political activities to address the negative race and gender images pervasive during her lifetime. The NCNW was chartered in the District of Columbia as a national women's organization specifically to lobby for the rights of African American women and children. In addition, her personal goals were to highlight the historical contributions, current capacity and future potential of African American women. She dedicated her life to addressing the neglected areas of accomplishment for her race all over the United States.

Although she was one of the most influential women of the twentieth century, Mary McLeod Bethune's contributions as an activist outside the United States are central to this book, which expands the diaspora themes and international policy actions impressively explored by many scholars today. As a co-founder of the International Council of Women of the Darker Races of the World, her leadership and policy development strategies affirm her focus on enhancing the condition of women and children of color in countries as diverse as Nigeria, Brazil, Puerto Rico, Haiti and the Philippines. Famed as an African American educator, the leader most well known for the creation of the National Council of Negro Women led reform efforts in Cuba and Liberia. As examples of her unparalleled respect in areas outside of the United States, Dr. Bethune was awarded the Haitian Medal of Honor in 1949 and the Medal of Africa in 1952.

Mary McLeod Bethune's spirit of literary inquiry is embedded in her writings. In her educational leadership texts, she encouraged all students to strive for good manners, a robust work ethic and a deep-seated respect for heritage. Her newspaper writings always called on readers to use positive actions to contend with obstacles. This leader invited readers to create appropriate responses to unjust actions grown out of ignorance.

As a person respected all over the world, her home was a place of refuge for international visitors, leaders from all over the United States and women from her surrounding communities. Mrs. Bethune adeptly advised leaders from all over the world on gender equality, counseled the president of the United States on equal employment opportunity and guided neighbors on characteristics of seed-bearing plants.

To quote Dr. Bethune, this work establishes her matchless determination to "invest in the human soul"; her courage to "change old ideas and practices so that we may direct their power toward good ends"; and a persistent belief that "knowledge is the prime need of the hour."

DR. ELIZABETH CLARK-LEWIS
Professor of History
Howard University

Preface

The condition of the African American woman presents a peculiar position. At the nexus of two marginalized groups—African Americans and women—her worldview provides her with a unique vision where humanity is able to breathe freely, harness their strengths and live full lives. Through collective action in the form of the club movements as well as via individual endeavors, these women made their voices heard. Thus, the extraordinary life of Mary McLeod Bethune—which spanned two centuries, two world wars and the Great Depression—contributed significantly to this tradition. She was an educator, race leader and humanitarian. This work examines the life of Bethune when she resided in Washington, D.C., from 1943 to 1949. During this brief window of time, she grew the National Council of Negro Women (NCNW) from a small organization intended for greatness into a national organization that became the leading voice of Negro women's activism/agency.

Bethune's life in Washington fulfilled a longstanding dream to house a national Negro women's organization in the nation's capital to lobby for the rights of Negro women and children. Moreover, the national headquarters served as the community space where the world could meet and engage Negro women as citizens. NCNW's house provided literal and figurative sanctuary for Negro women. The business affairs of the NCNW, such as publishing and mailing the *Telefact* newsletter, *Aframerican Women's Journal*, as well as housing the archives and library, provided the membership and visitors with information on the accomplishments of Negro women.

Moreover, the house provided an intangible sense of success and status for Negro women where international guests from Asia, Africa, Europe and the Caribbean were received and able to explore the history and culture of Negro womanhood as created and presented by themselves. The accommodations of the house, with bay windows, a grand piano and marble fireplace in the parlor, provided visitors a glimpse into the refinement of Negro women's tastes in America in the wake of enslavement and segregation. The house offered rooms for boarders, who were often lone Negro women traveling during a time when segregation did not provide adequate lodging.

Concurrently, Bethune maintained a room in the House as founder and president of the NCNW. She also maintained a residence in Daytona Beach, Florida, where she served as founder and president of Bethune Cookman College. She moved to Washington to assume the position as director of minority affairs for the National Youth Administration (NYA). She served the NYA from 1936 to 1943. In 1936, she incorporated the NCNW in Washington using the address of Howard University's Dean Lucy Diggs Slowe. Thus her position in Washington served a dual purpose of working for both the NYA and the NCNW. When NYA funding was cut in 1943, Bethune sought a place to live. Serendipitously, the NCNW was also searching for a property at this same time. While searching for private and organizational housing, she lived in several northwest locations, such as 316 T Street, 1812 Ninth Street, 1340 G Street, 2145 C Street and 1318 Vermont Avenue.

Washington during the waning years of the Great Depression was a southern town. Racial segregation was tacitly understood, while poverty was universally realized across racial lines. Bethune, a daughter of the south, understood the mores of segregation. However, by the 1930s, she opted to launch a frontal assault against the injustice that segregation placed on the shoulders of Negro women and girls. Living in Washington and directing NCNW afforded her an opportunity to realize her dreams of revealing the accomplishments and potential of Negro women to both domestic and international audiences.

While living in Washington, Bethune did not live her life apart from the local conditions of black people there. She sought to dismantle segregation. She participated with the New Negro Alliance "Don't Buy Where You Can't Work" campaigns, hoisting a picket sign along with longtime Washington residents. She took part in the National Negro Congress, and she also participated in the Citizens Committee on Race Relations with Wilbur La Roe Jr. and others. Bethune was concerned with the health and welfare of Negro women and children. The abusive treatment of a Negro woman denied admission to Sibley Hospital in a critical moment because of race resulted in Bethune protesting via petition with other prominent Washingtonians. She also engaged the Logan Circle community and area neighbors, such as historian Carter G. Woodson, Judge Marjorie M. Lawson, Congressman Adam Clayton Powell and others. She walked north to U Street, celebrating the victory of Joe Louis over Max Schmelling, and would walk south to the White House to meet with President Roosevelt.

From the NCNW Council House, Bethune sponsored programs such as the Honor Roll, an awards program that acknowledged women of all races in their respective efforts to usher in equality for women irrespective of race. The NCNW held Bethune birthday baseball games as fundraisers. She utilized her residency to promote the concerns and needs of Negro women. She became a Washingtonian and enjoyed the life and culture of black Washington. Toward the end of her residency in 1949, Bethune remarked about the need for home rule, a long-standing battle for Washingtonians throughout the twentieth century.

Many southerners have opposed home rule for the District of Columbia because they realized that with the power of the ballot, the local citizens, almost a third of who are Negroes, would make many needed changes. So, to the bill designed to give home rule by local suffrage, instead of a positive amendment to abolish segregation, the Dixiecrats took the initiative and introduced an amendment which would have made it next to impossible for the elected local representatives of the people of Washington to abolish segregation or enact any civil rights legislation. The fight in favor of home rule and against the amendment to preserve segregation was led by a southerner Senator Estes Kefauver of Tennessee...President Truman has given his backing to the anti-segregation fight...First-class citizenship is still not within our grasp. But while we have not yet grasped the victory banner, we can see it now on the hilltop, and we have all the more reason to climb...and keep moving forward.

Bethune's Washington years wrought changes in international, national and local policies that contributed to dismantling segregation. As a resident, she was fully involved in the local issues, people and institutions that comprised that community. Her leadership, celebrity and residency in Logan Circle inspired black women and girls throughout Washington who admired her tenacity and accomplishments. It is my hope that examining select activities of Bethune during her Washington residency will provide insight into the struggle for justice that she and other black Washingtonians sought while shadowed under the federal government. Georgia Douglas Johnson, a Washington poet, wrote of Bethune:

The world made way for you, your face
Became a Sessame, and then,
You reached the height, a smiling hill,
And, standing there, firm, and secure,
Reached down
With gentle, loving hand
To those who followed after you,
Who struggled up the cruel way—
Gave comfort, succor, cried aloud,
Come up, come on, stand by my side.

As the nation's capital, Washington attracted a host of political and celebrity residents, many of whom maintained property or housing in the city. Bethune utilized the city's status to her advantage and returned to the local community with solutions to injustice, segregation and unfair treatment. She understood the responsibility her leadership required. In a radio interview with WINX, Bethune said, "I always realize wherever I am that I am not representing myself alone, but the 15 million brown people of America...not only of my own people but of all the minorities—of all colonial people—who seek to be understood, and who crave a right to stand and be counted as one in the affairs of the world."

Acknowledgements

E very creative work is composed of suggestion and inspiration; this work is such a product. I would like to thank John Muller, who suggested I consider writing something for The History Press. His passion for local history prompted me to "look around" Washington and see what story needed telling. It also resulted in me obtaining a D.C. Public Library card providing me access to a wealth of black newspapers—a valuable source that is free and available to all residents. Thanks, John. Concurrently, Elaine Smith, Mrs. Bethune's biographer, completed a mammoth work on Bethune that highlighted aspects of her life untouched—one such aspect was her Washington years. Learning about Mrs. Bethune's coming to Washington in 1936 and maintaining a residence in Logan Circle was kismet. I have been to the Bethune Council House and had taken the tour but did not understand the gravity of what actually happened at 1318 Vermont Avenue until delving into the archives. The National Archives of Black Women's History is a rich source of primary sources documenting the activities of the NCNW as well as the affiliate organizations. Thank you, John and Elaine, for the suggestions; this work is a direct result of your contributions. Thank you to The History Press, and to Hannah Cassilly and Magan Thomas for sharing my journey into Mrs. Bethune's Washington.

I would like to thank the staff of the Mary McLeod Bethune Council House. Dr. Joy Kinard embraced the concept and offered me a number of angles to consider, while Margaret Miles shared her passion, offered insights about the House and served as a well-wisher on my journey. Archivist

Kenneth Chandler speedily delivered box after box, copy after copy and crisp images every time I requested materials. His willingness to provide assistance and his friendly service was remarkable. As scholars and colleagues, Tazwell Franklin, John Fowler II, Dr. Kimberly Brown and a host of others provided me with a positive research experience. I hope that this work will enrich the coffers of the Council House and reintroduce Mrs. Bethune to younger generations of Washingtonians.

I would like to thank Frances Lyons-Bristol, reference archivist of United Methodist Archives Center at Drew University. She responded quickly with a wealth of information held by no other institution. The materials answered a lot of questions and shed light on the value of Methodist archives in local history.

I would like to thank N. Adam Watson, photo archivist of the State Archives of Florida, for providing images of Mrs. Bethune. This collection holds some rare images of her early life. My colleagues at Moorland Spingarn have been tremendous. Thank you for everything. My fellow D.C. Historical Studies Conference committee burst with insightful tidbits about Washington life that contributed to the process of writing—many thanks.

Thanks to my parents, Enos Jones and Iris Jones; my uncle Ralph Greenidge; my sister, Marjorie Jones; and my nephews, Jay and Camar; as well as my friends Dr. Elizabeth Clark-Lewis, Dr. Richlyn F. Goddard, Milynda Williams and Shirley Gaither. They have all contributed through prayers and encouragement—the intangible things that keep you writing when bleary-eyed and tired. Thank you all.

I would like to posthumously thank Sue Bailey Thurman, Mary McLeod Bethune, Dorothy Porter Wesley, Carter G. Woodson and members of the NCNW archives committee. Their sensitivity in valuing the experience of our enslaved foremothers, the achievements of their contemporaries and the visions of future generations of black women is awe-inspiring. Their mission involved much collecting and interpreting of materials pertaining to the lives of Negro women. Mrs. Bethune wrote: "We want, through such a collection, to tell in concrete form the story of the contributions of Negro women to American life." I would like to thank the late Dr. Dorothy I. Height. She was indwelled with the mission of Mrs. Bethune and kept her alive in word, deed and dedication in securing the archives and the House.

Finally, I would like to thank my readers. This work contributes to the selfless heritage of black women, who historically seek to triangulate themselves in a yesterday, today and tomorrow in their own words for and about themselves. Enjoy.

Introduction

The lives of African American people from 1890 to 1954 were plagued with legalized segregation as mandated through the 1896 Supreme Court decision in *Plessy vs. Ferguson*, which ruled that separate accommodations in public, educational and social settings were not inherently inferior. Therefore, it was determined that blacks and whites need not attend the same schools, churches and businesses or live in the same neighborhoods. The *Plessy* decision did not take into account the deprivation and economic imbalance African Americans incurred through two hundred years of chattel enslavement. Legalized segregation was accompanied by violence and extralegal measures to keep African American citizens in communities that were secluded both physically and intellectually.

This is the America that Bethune came of age in as a resident of South Carolina. Bethune and her contemporaries did not allow the limitations of the *Plessy* decision or the subsequent violent attacks against them to constrict their dreams of embracing the possibilities entitled to all American citizens. Select members of Bethune's generation attended and built schools, created organizations and were mentored and sought to mentor rising generations of African American children. For Bethune, doing these things was an honor and a Christian duty to lift the race out of degradation. Her life was a yardstick to measure the progress of one generation and a mirror to reflect the possibilities to younger generations.

As a child, Mary Jane McLeod Bethune experienced two things that impressed her so deeply that she lived her life in pursuit of attaining them. One was intangible, and the other was a material aesthetic: honesty in character and a home with glass windows. Affectionately called Mary Jane by family, she was connected to both of her parents and expressed love for them equally. However, her father, Samuel McLeod, allowed her to accompany him to the cotton scales, where they exchanged raw cotton for cash. During those trips, she was gifted with candy and other treats. The trips were bonding times between father and daughter. On one trip, she recalled her father shielding her from being a witness to a fight that turned into a lynching. The white and black men disagreed, and "slumbering hatred flamed." All she remembered were her father's instructions not to look back while he placed her in the mule-drawn cart.

As she grew older and enrolled in school, she helped her father and other black farmers avoid being shortchanged by the cotton purchasers. Moreover, many of the black people selling cotton were formerly enslaved and had never been taught to read, so they simply accepted the prices quoted in deference to survival and a viable livelihood. When she corrected the cotton merchant, he accepted her correction—often with snide remarks—but usually measured and paid correct amounts. The trips to the cotton merchant reinforced in her young mind the desire to become someone who does not cheat or take advantage of others, as she had felt the sting of being shortchanged and did not like it. Also, her ability to help people stemmed from learning, so education resulted in honesty in her mind. In her later years, she stated, "Power must walk hand in hand with humility, and the intellect must have a soul." Thus, she committed herself to living a life pursuing education and honesty in order to aid those less fortunate.

When returning home from the cotton merchant, she and her father would pass big homes owned by white people. Those homes were unlike the cabin her family lived in because these homes had glass windows. She was not embarrassed by their living accommodations, however. After all, her father had built the cabin, and as a result, the family of nearly twenty was sheltered from the elements. Nevertheless, the McLeod home had wooden shutters that did not allow for light to enter. She longed to live in a house with windows of glass rather than wooden panels. This detail represented progress and higher social status within her community since all white people did not live like those in the large houses. Moreover, she thought her parents would enjoy being able to sit safely inside and look outside through glass windows. Toward this end, she committed herself as well as the organizations she stewarded to own property—preferably with glass windows but most importantly, property that was owned and occupied by

Negro women. Property ownership provided safety and wholeness, which Reconstruction America and, later, segregated cities did not afford Negro people. Thus, her life's motto was the pursuit of education and honesty, as well as owning property, privately and corporately. These aspects of her character are evident throughout her private and professional life.

Her grandmother Sophia; parents, Samuel and Patsy McLeod; and older siblings were originally enslaved and never had the chance to own property until the end of enslavement. There were black families that owned property prior to the Civil War, but the vast majority of black people were enslaved and had to wait for the Emancipation Proclamation and passage of the Thirteenth, Fourteenth and Fifteenth Amendments to enjoy the liberty to pursue property ownership. The McLeod family worked hard and purchased five acres of land and acquired another thirty through thrift and cooperation. They grew cotton and rice for sale and consumption. There were rabbits, possum, apples, peaches and other food sources on their land. The humble beginnings on the McLeods' farm, called the Homestead, provided fond memories, a sense of safety and landscaping aesthetics that she carried into her adult life.

Education was the desire of Bethune's generation, and many schools opened through Christian philanthrophy; many of the early schools in need of land aquired plots through church purchase or government land grants. In 1904, she opened the Daytona Normal School and grew the campus from a boarding elementary school to an accredited four-year college—all begun from $1.50 and a dream of offering an education to young Negro girls. Bethune's vision of education for Negro girls eventually expanded to include boys and parents. The community uplift propelled her into positions of authority and leadership. Bethune's humility and passion fueled her leadership positions with charismatic, sincere and enduring opportunities. One such opportunity was the chance to be a voice for Negro people in Washington.

On May 19, 1928, in an open letter as president of the National Association of Colored Women (NACW), she persuaded the organization to purchase a national headquarters building as a way of establishing a permanent presence in Washington. The building was not simply for operational purposes, which would benefit the organization, but it would also become a living shrine to the progress and posterity of colored women.

We must assuredly build for ourselves and posterity. Only today is ours.
The future is for our children...I, Mary McLeod Bethune, in light of

my own experience see the colored women of these 48 states and the one district of these United States circling around a center—the District—the hub of the government of our country where the laws are made, where the Departmental Bureau governing every phase of our lives are operated, this center from which must come the decisions that will lift from us the curse of inferiority even as we lift ourselves; this center from which we shall force ourselves upon the notice of our government, so that it will recognize our worth and repay our efforts; this center which will put us in touch with international groups and problems and, in which we can be reached, and acknowledged as a factor in the problems of the world. My friend, do you now see why we must have our Headquarters, and in Washington and as close to government buildings as possible?

The NACW founded in 1896 was composed of educated women who sought to ameliorate poor racial conditions in their states and regions. The numerous regional organizations consolidated into a national body to share strategies and strength in the struggle for equality. The NACW opted to address issues regionally and model examples of acceptable behavior. The *Plessy* decision gave court-approved racial discrimination an opportunity to flourish, which was compounded when gender was a factor. Bethune understood the NACW membership and their position. Still, she pressed forward, writing:

If the N.A.C.W. and its branches regional, state and city are to function properly and to become permanent lighthouses, guardians and protectors, disseminators of social knowledge to our group, they must be fixed and operated so as to demand the confidence of our municipal governments so that they in turn will accept the N.A.C.W. and its branches as agents for the distribution of funds to the poor, the indigent, the incorrigible. These same governments will recognize their duty to our group when we demonstrate to them that we are united upon one program and are competent and sufficiently interested...As we accept responsibilities for the welfare of our group and we operate before the world a well regulated definite, tangible machine, this same world will mete out to us in larger measures its confidence its respect and its funds?

Bethune had envisioned the NACW headquarters as a business office; publication facility; "haven of security and comfort" for black women visiting Washington; an archives for NACW; a home for women and girls attending Howard University; a place where the government and peoples from all over the world "may contact colored women of these United States as a whole"; and "a fountainhead, a source, a heart pulsating with the warm blood of 250,000 colored women scattered from the Great Lakes to the Gulf and from the Atlantic to the Pacific."

The NACW purchased its national headquarters at Twelfth and O Streets, Northwest, in 1928. Bethune believed this purchase was a move in the right direction. In the late 1920s, the New Negro movement utilized art and literature to speak to a new identity. This mistreatment of soldiers after World War I allowed a generation of young people more room to express their displeasure with being treated as second-class citizens. African Americans had fought in every war and shed their blood for the ideals of democracy. America spread democracy across the globe, yet it denied their sable citizens. No longer was this acceptable. Bethune, a seasoned educator, believed that collective action and a visible presence in Washington were essential to destroying segregation. Unfortunately, the leadership of the NACW retreated, in part because of the impending economic crisis: the Great Depression. It streamlined the organization from twenty-two programs into two. The NACW focused on local and regional self-help projects as well as maintenance of the Douglass home.

Conversely, Bethune viewed the 1930s as a time of opportunity. In December 1935, she—along with fellow educators, club women and activists like college president Charlotte Hawkins Brown, NACW founder Mary Church Terrell, reformer Addie Dickinson and civil rights activist Daisy Lampkin—organized the National Council of Negro Women. Bethune was elected the first president. From its inception until her death in 1955, Bethune and the NCNW were inseparable.

Bethune's vision and charisma attracted a number of young women whose education and desire for inclusion required an organization that would allow them voice and participation. With the NCNW, Bethune envisioned a channel through which women with greater advantages shared their professional training and expertise with each other. Young women, such as lawyer Sadie T.M. Alexander, social worker Dorothy I. Height and educator Edna Forrest Brown pooled their talents and galvanized their professional and organizational connections to advance the agenda of the NCNW. Bethune implored Council women "not to view themselves as a selective group but as a great, forceful, inclusive group with roots solidly in the group, drawing from the soil of the mass people the nourishment to sustain our growth, broaden our vision, and extend our service." The NCNW's purchase of 1318

Vermont Avenue cemented the presence of Negro women in the nation's capital. Moreover, Bethune's stature as an NAACP Spingarn medal award winner and federal government appointee in the Roosevelt administration with ties to white philanthropies and influence with the Negro women's club movement provided her a unique position as stateswoman.

This work examines how Bethune's Washington residency, her political power and humanitarian passions melded together from 1943 to 1949. The work is composed of five chapters. Each chapter explores an aspect of Bethune's life, from her earliest childhood memories to her evolution into a de facto elder stateswoman to her persistent desire to see Negro people and other marginalized groups experience full civil rights. The twin desires for honesty and education and her love for glass windows provide an example of the simplicity in Bethune's personal life. Concurrently, her life's mission sought to provide Negro women and girls the latitude to realize their potential and envision a world where peace and equality were possible.

The impact of Bethune's Washington years can never fully be quantified. For example, Loretta Carter Hanes, a Washingtonian, attended Lucretia Mott Elementary School and recalled meeting Bethune. "All these people came in person, like Mary McLeod Bethune. They came in person to inspire you...They all embraced you and loved you and inspired you to do your best and your very best. They [select whites] had everything and we had nothing, but we had people to inspire us and they taught us how to struggle. We were taught whatever you do, don't be ashamed of the job that you do." Hanes blossomed into a local activist who singlehandedly salvaged the history of Washington's Emancipation Day celebrations. Hanes remarked that encountering the elderly Bethune infused her with a sense of wanting to become someone similar.

There are countless stories recorded and remembered about Bethune's Washington years. This work seeks to present a snapshot of Bethune's life from her earliest childhood memories and focusing in detail on the record of select events from 1943 to 1949 when her dream of showcasing Negro women in Washington and providing a viable mirror for younger women to see their potential reflected lived at 1318 Vermont Avenue.

CHAPTER 1

Mary Jane McLeod

The life of Bethune can be divided into two parts: pre-NCNW and post-NCNW. This chapter will examine her family roots; formation of the Daytona Industrial School; her advocacy for boys, girls and women as an emerging leader; leadership in NACW; formation of NCNW; and the encounter with the Roosevelt women. The first four ingredients formed the vision and strength Bethune used to promote racial equality and pursue civil rights for women, while the last two serve as manifestations of her civil rights dreams. Education was the greatest gift of emancipation. The opportunity, promise and capacity to learn motivated many formerly enslaved people to send their children to school as well as seek personal instruction for themselves, no matter how rudimentary. Thus, the motto of her school—"Give them a chance"—begged of potential donors to give the female children of formerly enslaved people a chance. Her life modeled the benefits of a chance investment made in her education, and she sought to provide such for other girls.

HER FAMILY ROOTS

Mary McLeod Bethune was born the fifteenth child of her parents' seventeen children, but unlike her older siblings, she was born free on July 10, 1875. Her parents, Samuel and Patsy McLeod, were slaves. Samuel was reared on the McLeod plantation, thus his last name. Patsy believed Mary to be different from her other children because she was born with her eyes wide open. According to one biography, the midwife declared, "She's different, Patsy. She'll see things before they happen." Samuel and Patsy McLeod nurtured the innate inquisitiveness of young Mary. The freedom Bethune experienced in childhood by happenstance of being born free contributed to her being able to think and dream bigger than her enslaved family members. Her big dreams remained an aspect of her character for life. As Rackham Holt wrote in *Mary McLeod Bethune: A Biography*, she was "free to think and dream and plan and become the woman leader of her race; always grateful that she came into the world thus, with an inner confidence nothing could ever shake." The McLeods were an industrious family and purchased land where Samuel and his sons built a cabin for the family. The cabin, dubbed the Homestead, stood on a rising plot of land protected by the boughs of enormous oak trees. The farm was orderly and the buggy functional. Samuel erected other structures on the property as the family needed, including a wash shed equipped with tubs, a storehouse and a smokehouse where meats were seasoned.

Patsy utilized her skills in carding and spinning cotton to make clothes for the family. She also maintained a grapevine and fig tree. Holt wrote that the McLeods were Christian people, and Patsy referred to Micah 4:4, which references a vine and fig tree. During enslavement, the luxury of being able to sit when one wanted to was not available, but after the Civil War, Patsy enjoyed being able to sit under her own vine and fig tree. Fresh fruit, fish and small game provided nourishment for the McLeod family. The nutritional food was augmented by emotional sustenance in the stories of survival during enslavement from her grandmother, parents and elder sister Sallie. As Holt wrote, many times Mary heard the story of slavery from the lips of formerly enslaved people. During enslavement, faith became an integral part of life and subsequently a part of Mary's life, providing her resilience and fortitude. The stories of survival and faith reaffirmed in her mind the importance of personally acknowledging and knowing God. Faith in God manifested itself in prayer and singing, all of which Mary integrated into her life's plan.

She viewed herself as destined for greatness according the Lord's plan for her life. One day, when accompanying her mother as she delivered laundry to a white family she worked for, Mary was reprimanded for touching the books in the house. One of the white girls informed her that she could not read and should not touch the books. Young Mary could not understand why some people were allowed to read and others not. She realized that school

Samuel and Patsy McIntosh McLeod were the parents of Mary McLeod Bethune. *Courtesy of State Archives of Florida.*

offered the possibility of learning, which would erase all differences between her and her white counterparts. Mary prayed to God asking for someone to teach her to read and write. Ms. Emma Wilson and Reverend J.C. Simmons were the answer to Mary's prayers. Wilson and Simmons were sent by the Board of Missions for Freedmen of the Trinity Presbyterian Church to open a school in Mayesville and called on the McLeod family seeking children to enroll. Her parents allowed her to attend school, and Mary absorbed all she could. Learning was easy for her.

Her first lesson in Ms. Wilson's class was John 3:16, which reads, "For God so loved that world that He gave His only begotten Son, that whosoever believeth in Him should not perish, but have everlasting life." The "whosoever" provided her exclusive access to God because he saw her as an individual and special creation. She believed that God created her and everyone else equally with a unique purpose and destiny. This scripture reaffirmed her faith. Her mother's simple and practical faith infused young

Mary with a sense of confidence and self-esteem. Mary cleaved to the John 3:16 verse. As a child, she was called homely. However, the self-esteem and confidence she received from her parents, reinforced by scripture, allowed the painful taunts of being dubbed "uncomely" to bounce off young Mary. She did not believe herself unattractive. Ms. Wilson's deportment and soft manner also impressed Mary greatly. Never before had she seen an African American woman move in such a fashion, and her mannerisms influenced Mary, leading her to possibly mimic her behavior.

Education fostered Mary's leadership abilities. She created a children's savings account measure called the Tin Can Banking Circle. Mary was the banker, and she advised other children how to save their pennies and not buy candy frivolously. It was important to be thrifty. Delayed gratification allowed for better Christmas presents and greater charity. She also organized a Mouth Organ Band where she served as the band master while allowing other children room to share their musical gifts as well.

Her childhood was not without episodes of ugly racism and violence. When she would return home, poor white children threatened her and pelted her with rocks. Patsy implored Mary to confront the bullies and stand up for herself, explaining that if she continued to run they would never stop tormenting her. She confronted the bullies, and they stopped their torment. Naïve and trusting, she grew affectionate toward a young man whose intentions Patsy believed impure. Samuel and Patsy viewed their investment in Mary as too great to be squandered on inappropriate male attention. Patsy explained to her that every decision had a consequence. All persons interested her were not benefical to her, and she needed to weigh the current moment against the potential of her future. Mary obeyed her parents.

At age twelve, Mary graduated from the Presbyterian Church school. During the graduation ceremony, Reverend J.W.E. Bowen of Atlanta, Georgia, told stories of his missionary trips to Africa. Mary felt moved to do missionary work, preferably in Africa. Like her mentors Ms. Wilson and Reverend Simmons, Mary decided that she too would become a missionary and repay her obligation to mankind. The fruit of her obedience opened the doors to more education. Ms. Wilson located Ms. Mary Chrissman, a Quaker seamstress who sought to use her earnings to benefit a needy student. Wilson immediately thought of Mary and her own alma mater of Scotia Seminary in Concord, North Carolina. In 1887, with tears, prayers, handshakes and clapping, Mary left the Homestead for her first journey into the world beyond Mayesville.

Mary McLeod Bethune lived in this Mayesville cabin. Rachel and Maria, Bethune's sisters, are in front of the cabin. *Courtesy of State Archives of Florida.*

Mary's train ride to Concord was a heady experience. She viewed her first brick building, plastered walls and glass windows. The tables were covered with white tablecloths, napkins and water glasses. Her first dinner was at long tables where blacks and whites sat side by side. Scotia principal Dr. David J. Satterfield informed the new students of the school motto: "Not to be ministered unto but to minister." The school emphasized the head, the heart and the hand. This idea of tempered and principle learning remained an element of Mary's life. Her student life was punctual and utilitarian. She often worked during school breaks to subsidize her school fees. She sought to make herself indispensable, thus ensuring her opportunity to remain and learn more. Mary made the school a home-like environment. Her leadership skills propelled her into a position as mediator between faculty and students. As Holt explained in Mary's biography, "She had the right voice for it as well as the ear of the teachers...[Students] felt they had a right to protest these things. The teachers had trained them in their independence of spirit and encouraged it. But they needed a spokesman." Mary enjoyed a social life and was known to sing and dance. Still, her life's purpose of being a missionary kept her tethered to a sense of serious-mindedness. Moreover, her sponsor, Ms. Chrissman, received regular reports about her grades.

While at Scotia, Mary received faculty assistance in seeking admissions to Moody Bible Institute in Chicago, and in 1894, she was admitted. At nearly nineteen years old, Mary was the only African American student among the thousands at Moody. Her initial missionary work was in an impoverished Chicago neighborhood on Clark Street. The rowdy people were not interested or receptive to Mary's evangelical message. That incident did not deter her, and she pressed on, seeking to become the missionary to Africa as envisioned by her twelve-year-old self. While at the institute, Mary had the pleasure of meeting school founder Dwight Moody. His sermon during a New Year's Eve service inspired the students to seek power from the Holy Spirit, though Moody's theology on the Holy Spirit was not fully embraced by most Protestant denominations. Moody believed the Holy Spirit empowered believers with supernatural authority to accomplish the Lord's will on earth. Mary knew she needed the power of the Holy Spirit, and she wanted to have power over men and women to influence them to choose justice over injustice. When she completed her instruction at Moody, she applied to the Mission Board of the Presbyterian Church asking to be assigned to "somewhere in Africa." The answer from the Mission Board was that no openings were available for Negro missionaries in Africa. Disheartened, Mary returned to Mayesville for one year and taught as an assistant to Ms. Wilson. She then requested another assignment from the Presbyterian Board of Education and was assigned to the Haines Institute in Augusta, Georgia.

The Haines Normal and Industrial Institute was founded by Lucy Craft Laney, who was born in 1864 in Macon, Georgia. Her father was a deeply religious man who co-founded the John Knox Presbytery in 1868. It was the first all-black Presbyterian Synod in the United States. Her mother was enslaved by the Campbell family, where Ms. Campbell taught Laney to read. She was a schoolteacher who appointed Laney the caretaker of her library. Ms. Campbell facilitated Laney's attendance to Atlanta University at the age of fifteen years old. She graduated in 1873 at the head of her class and immediately entered the profession of teaching. Laney enjoyed the challenges of public school teaching, but when the Presbyterian Board of Missions started a private school, Laney took the position. Unfortunately, the Board of Missions did not provide for the full funding of the school, and Laney had to raise additional monies. In 1886, she founded her own school for girls in Augusta, Georgia. However, when the bedraggled boys arrived, she allowed them to enroll as well. Laney counted on tuition fees to support the school. Unfortunately, the volume of children often came without tuition payments. She traveled to the Presbyterian board meeting to request funding, but she received only moral support, not the necessary financial assistance.

Despite this obstacle, Laney redoubled her efforts to combat illiteracy in Georgia, where 36.5 percent of the one million African American residents could not read. Laney realized that, though college preparation was the end goal, kindergarten and formative education was a more pressing need for the majority of her students. In 1893, the school provided boarding and furnishing for sixty to seventy girls and fifteen to twenty boys in rented cottages. Laney's school provided a living laboratory for Mary, whose missionary dreams morphed into the desire to become an educator. Laney reached out to ambitious students regardless of their financial circumstances. Thus, Mary dreamed of becoming a missionary through being an educator. Many of the students did not have much materially, and northern missionary barrels provided proper clothing, though it was often in need of mending. Holt states, "Her constant endeavor was to shore up her people, to instill the vital spark of aspiration and confidence in their innate abilities to emerge from the slough in which they were mired." Mary believed education was the stepping stone for African American people to enable them to emerge from under the stigma of racism and poverty. Her own life provided an example, and the life of Lucy Laney did the same. Within a year, she left Haines Institute for Sumter, South Carolina, to work at the Kindell Institute.

Although Mary did not remain at the Homestead, she still contributed to her family. When the family mule died, the cost of a new one resulted in remortgaging the Homestead. Mary contributed to the bill and aided the family in paying off the debt. While in Sumter, she joined a church and sang in the choir. During choir rehearsal, she met Albertus Bethune. He was attentive, gallant and handsome and taught her how to ride a bicycle. Bethune was a teacher who left the profession because it was underpaid. He worked in a department store and used part of his income to send his brother to school. Mary and Albertus courted for one year, after which she brought her prospective groom to the Homestead. Her parents approved, and in May 1898, Albertus and Mary were married by Reverend J.C. Watkins, principal of Kindell Institute. Within the first year of marriage, they moved to Savannah, Georgia, and in February 1899, Albertus McLeod Bethune Jr. was born. When Albertus Jr. was nine months old, Mary traveled to Palatka, Florida, to start a parochial school at the suggestion of Palatka pastor Reverend C.J. Uggans.

The early years of her marriage were strained under the burden of building the school. Albertus's wages and Mary's income from the Mission School required that she augment their finances through selling insurance policies, which also contributed to the school's growth. Growing the mission school opened a private desire within Mary to have her own school. To provide an education for girls thrilled Mary. Albertus wanted to be a businessman himself, yet he did not curtail Mary's dream. Unfortunately, they eventually grew apart and separated. He moved back to South Carolina while she built her school in Daytona Beach.

One biography states that Mrs. Bethune had a dream in which she was standing on the brink of the St. John's River and had to cross over. No bridge or boat was in sight. When she looked behind her, there was a great army of young people coming after her. A man in the dream handed her a notebook and pencil. He said all must pay to cross over, saying, "You are going to cross over this river, but before you go, you must write down the names of all the young people you see in the distance." Her pastor interpreted the dream as symbolizing her destiny of being a school builder where thousands of young people would pass through her hands.

FORMATION OF THE DAYTONA INDUSTRIAL SCHOOL: "GIVE THEM A CHANCE"

Mrs. Bethune embraced the dream of establishing a school for Negro girls, and she sought direction from various sources. The leadership in Palatka wanted her to stay there and build on the existing foundation, but Mrs. Bethune wanted to start her school in virgin territory. Reverend S.P. Pratt suggested she go to Daytona, fifty miles south of Palatka. Daytona attracted a number of wealthy white people, and the Florida East Coast Railway was building up the area. The combination of Negro workers and their families along with wealthy white travelers assured potential students and financial donors. Mrs. Bethune headed to Daytona. Reverend Pratt suggested she contact Mrs. Susie Warren, who offered her a tour of

Mary McLeod Bethune, circa 1904. *Courtesy of State Archives of Florida.*

Left: Daytona Educational and Industrial Training School for Girls brochure, circa 1905. *Courtesy of Moorland Spingarn Research Center, Ethel Payne Papers.*

Below: Reverse image from Daytona Educational and Industrial Training School for Girls brochure, circa 1905. *Courtesy of Moorland Spingarn Research Center, Ethel Payne Papers.*

Our community work with children and adults has help to raise the "rounded standard" of the community.

Daytona. Mrs. Bethune's declaration of her intent to start a school for Negro girls piqued Mrs. Warren's interest because she had three daughters and one son. The schools for Negro children were open only a few months a year, and a white women's philanthropic group, the Palmetto Club, sponsored a kindergarten for Negro children to avoid latch-key situations. Mary continued to experience prophetic dreams, and all answers seemingly pointed to Daytona: "[t]he need among the workmen's families; the possibilities for raising funds to sustain the school; the paradise of trees, gray bearded yet perpetually renewing their youth," according to Holt. The trees reminded her of the Homestead and the sanctuary they provided from the elements as well as the biblical symbolism of deliverance from enslavement as experienced by her mother. She selected a two-story frame building on Palm Street near the railroad and rented the place for eleven dollars a month. After securing housing, Mrs. Bethune returned to Palatka, where a fire had destroyed her home. She collected her son and salvageable belongs and moved to Daytona.

The humble and meager building on Palm Street lacked most everything needed to start a school. However, Mrs. Bethune's faith and prayers inspired her to press on and open the school. She used boxes and packing crates as chairs and desks. On October 4, 1904, Mrs. Bethune declared the Daytona Educational and Industrial Training School for Negro Girls in session with five students: Lucille, Lena, Ruth, Anna and Celeste. The inaugural school day opened with a prayer asking the Lord's blessing and a hymn, "Leaning on the Everlasting Arms." The early faculty was composed of older adult women who could read and were willing to volunteer. The children were daughters of working women whose chief concern had been the safety of their daughters. The first boarding students were three little girls whose mother was kept late at work. Mrs. Bethune crafted mattresses from sun-dried Spanish moss. Although the neighborhood was poor, many in the neighborhood supported the activities of the school. Soon Mrs. Bethune also offered evening classes to adults. Sunday afternoons were open houses for cultural and historical lessons. The meager resources were augmented by everything from recycling used furniture from local hotels to cast-off food from area farms.

Mrs. Dora E. Maley was the first white woman to make a contribution when she purchased Mrs. Bethune's son a pair of mittens. This act of kindness led Mrs. Bethune to approach the Palmetto Club on behalf of the school. Mrs. Maley served as the president of the advisory board that secured funds, food and clothing for students. Mrs. Bethune conducted door-to-door campaigns on behalf of her school, and she always used prayer and faith to undergird her endeavors. One Christmas Eve, the dishes she intended to use were recalled by the owner for another use. The students queried how they were to eat without any plates. Mrs. Bethune told them the Lord would provide. In the final stages of preparation for their dinner, a gentleman delivered a set of dishes at exactly the right time.

Mrs. Bethune sought greater sums of money to ensure continuity at the school. Her first large donor was James M. Gamble, of Procter and Gamble in Cincinnati, Ohio. Gamble had a winter house in the Daytona area. She wrote him a letter about the school and met with him to discuss her request that he become a trustee of her school. She sought his advice, influence and direction. Gamble joined Laurence Thompson, E.L. Smith and African American ministers A.L. James and Reverend Cromatia. These men agreed to serve the school as the board of trustees. Gamble was the chairman, Thompson the treasurer and James the secretary. The first decision of the board was the purchase of land known as Hell's Hole, an area on the fringes of a black settlement. Gamble employed his own attorney Bert Fish, who contributed his legal services without cost.

Mrs. Bethune's school grew in tandem with her ideas on how to raise money. She approached Mrs. Howard of the Howard Hotel and invited her to visit the school to see if she would endorse it. Mrs. Howard and Mrs. Bethune agreed that a quartet of singers could perform Negro spirituals and folk songs in the hotel to solicit funds. The first performance netted $150. She approached other hotels and had success performing similar works. Another benefactor to the school was Thomas H. White of Cleveland, Ohio, the president of White Sewing Machine Company and the manufacturer of the White Steamer automobiles. He encountered Mrs. Bethune's students during a hotel concert. He visited the school and provided carpenters and masons to finish construction of Faith Hall. White also provided bed linens and blankets, and he exerted extra pressure in favor of Mrs. Bethune's request for public utilities for her school. The school's provision offered the entire Negro community the benefit of modern living and safeguards to health.

By 1916, Mrs. Bethune received her mother on campus. In Holt's biography of Bethune, he states, "A crowing joy shed its radiance upon her as she drove in the smartly polished buggy to welcome her mother. When they arrived at the school, all the girls lined up in their uniforms, standing at attention to greet Mrs. Patsy McLeod...One of the rooms had been especially painted, finished and decorated for her."

Above: Mary McLeod Bethune with a line of girls from the school, circa 1905. *Courtesy of State Archives of Florida.*

Left: Mary M. Bethune, principal, circa 1910–1911. *Courtesy of State Archives of Florida.*

The school eventually transcended its original purpose of education for Negro girls and became a center of interracial culture and goodwill throughout Daytona. The success of the school opened doors in northern cities. Mrs. Bethune's first trip was to Pittsburgh at the invitation of Mr. Mellour. Mrs. Bethune spoke with sincerity and spiritual depth. She informed potential donors of the progress students were making and explained that their donations would benefit American society through making educated citizens of her students. The Pittsburgh trip opened doors to Massachusetts and New York. The contributions were generous, but more important than the contributions were the contacts and friendships Mrs. Bethune made during her northern visits.

While in New York, she met Mrs. Frances R. Keyser, who operated the White Rose Mission settlement home. Mrs. Bethune and Mrs. Keyser shared a vision of a better life for young Negro women. Mrs. Keyser was recruited by Mrs. Bethune and joined the faculty of the Daytona School and introduced Mrs. Bethune to the National Association of Colored Women. The NACW was meeting in Hampton, Virginia. At the women's gathering were older and established leaders, such as Mrs. Booker T. Washington and Mary Church Terrell. A mixture of awe and intimidation overcame Mrs. Bethune, but she used the power of observation to learn from those accomplished women. She gave a note to the president asking for five minutes to speak about her school. She was granted the five minutes, and her presentation so moved the august body that it raised a collection for her school.

Mrs. Bethune believed the purpose of education was not merely to attain a degree but also to cultivate the whole human. Thus, the motto of her school's home economic department: "Cease to be a drudge; seek to be an artist." Skill in handicrafts was essential for those who would not teach or operate their own businesses.

The connotation between manual labor and the Negro woman stripped these women of their femininity, softness and beauty. The idea of being a household engineer and domestic artist moved Negro women from being solely working women to women who work. Bethune privately nursed the idea of respectability and refinement in her personal appearance and influenced her student charges with similar aesthetics. Moreover, her northern travels resulted in learning by personal witness the variety available in Negro women's leadership. The women of the NACW were educated, pedigreed and highly cultured, especially in the northeastern part of the country. At times aloof and cool, many of the club women were connected to other women through church, educational and, at times, marital relationships. Bethune, socially unpedigreed and from meager beginnings, resolved to remain a humble servant of the Lord doing his work to help other little girls rise beyond their circumstances. This spiel motivated people to donate to her vision of education for racial betterment. Her dedication, passion and simplicity in pursuing a better way of life for all Negro girls and women provided the right formula to propel her into leadership within the NACW, and Bethune's humility, articulate speech and passion placed her before larger audiences of influential women.

Advocate for Boys, Girls and Women

Bethune and others of her generation believed that education was the initial step into full American citizenship. Once the Negro was educated, he or she could influence others and seek to claim a place at the table of American democracy and brotherhood. Bethune's early education at Scotia Seminary and influence by Booker T. Washington led her to believe that social activism was an outgrowth of a good education. The Christian principle of being one's brother's keeper impelled those who had access to better to share the wealth of their betterment with the less fortunate. Her childhood and the street scenes in Daytona drove her to live that message. The images of poor, underfed, restless youth resulted in an invitation to the surrounding community of the Daytona School to come to the campus on Sundays for refreshment and moral instruction. "Lemonade, ginger snaps, and peanuts were spread on tables while she talked, pointed out that Negro boys, like white boys could become dependable, responsible citizens," according to Holt's biography of Bethune.

She provided surrogate relationships with neighborhood boys, showing them constructive ways to spend their time. This endeavor resulted in the Better Boys Club (BBC). The BBC provided reading and study halls as well as social games, using objectives similar to the YMCA. Bethune implored a civic-minded white man building a YMCA for white children to aid in her effort with Negro boys. Although the help did not come, many of the BBC children influenced their communities. One such product of the BBC was Dr. Howard Thurman Dean of Howard University's Chapel.

Bethune's care for the neighborhood children also extended to their families. In 1907, she formed the Tomoka Mission. The mission was a project that gathered children together while the mothers were given instructions in new domestic science and nursing innovations. The sense of community ownership endeared her school to local residents, and Bethune increased in stature within local affairs throughout Daytona. Bethune used her campus as an interracial, nondenominational meeting place for people to gather and discuss local affairs. Her use of the campus for such matters displeased many segregationists, who threatened to march on the campus and destroy the buildings. Through prayer and planning, Bethune's campus was spared destruction, and each threat was always neutralized by the stalwart prayers of Mrs. Bethune.

Her influence provided economic improvement as well. The students learned marketable skills and made handicrafts. The hand, heart and head concept placed students in working farms and gardens during their academic preparation. The usefulness of being able to grow a garden or maintain a farm directly benefitted the students, whose meals were enriched through their own efforts. Moreover, employment and sellable items provided students with multiple streams of income, which in turn benefitted the school and ultimately benefitted the students in their future lives. The handicrafts and extra produce were sold at school bazaars, providing tangible examples of the school's usefulness.

Holt explains that local women were attracted to Bethune's doggedness. "Women of both races were inclined to recognize her as the universal woman and follow her leadership without question. Her appeal to the men, also of both races, who became her admirers, followers, and supporters, was mixed with the appeal of her femininity and respect for what they would have called her masculine type of mind—she thought as clearly and decisively as any man, with no fumbling. Whatever the motivation, only those who had a kindred impulse toward stretching out a helping hand to the helpless would have been attracted into her orbit."

There were numerous donors that Bethune kept record of in her log. Of note was Mrs. Curtis, who bequeathed $20,000 in 1920 to the school with the stipulation that fresh flowers adorn her grave site in Buffalo, New York. Mr. Peabody donated $10,000 after hearing a student's recitation. Mr. Harrison Rhodes visited the campus and joined the trustee board. He invested time in visiting classrooms, convened with the Tomoka Mission and met with teachers. His assessment resulted in contacting the Carnegie Foundation for a grant to purchase books. The request was favorably answered, and the library became a central feature on the fledgling campus. Moreover, the free library provided the general public with a new opportunity. Bethune's pleasure with the library resulted in seeking to meet wealthy northern donors by introduction of Mr. Rhodes. Bethune met Orme Wilson, sister of Vincent Astor, at her home in New York. Wilson provided fifty guests for Bethune's presentation, including members of the Guggenheim, Vanderbilt and Pierpont families and others. Bethune utilized this time to display handicrafts made by the students as she spoke of the progress students made academically. She shared her vision with the audience of a place where the child lowest on the social ladder could rise out of the depths of ignorance and poverty if only given a chance. This presentation endeared her to members of these philanthropic families, whose interest moved from her school to her person, and friendship blossomed from the initial encounter. Her influence grew to include junior and senior Rockefellers. Their personal wealth and large influence expontially benefitted the school.

Within ten years of its opening, the Daytona School graduated its first classes of eighth graders. One student, Arabella Denniston, remained with Bethune and attended to her as a personal secretary, traveling with her from Florida to Washington. Bethune, unsatisfied with only an eighth grade curriculum, expanded and included a high school. In 1915, the first high school class graduated.

Within those same ten years, the near death of one student from appendicitis resulted in Bethune opening a hospital on campus. Miles from the Negro hospital, the ill student was given care on the back porch of a white doctor's house. As the student population grew, potential health crises would increase, and segregated treatment and no substantive hospital for Negroes in Daytona bothered Bethune. She was not without medical advice, however. Dr. T.A. Adams attended Meharry Medical College in Nashville, Tennessee, and returned to his parents' home in Daytona. Since 1905, Dr. Adams had provided medical care to people throughout the community, and he desired his own hospital. Bethune and Dr. Adams outfitted a campus cottage with two hospital beds and Bibles. Gamble and White, as well as other white donors, contributed to the hospital. The two beds grew to twenty-six, and white doctors contributed their expertise. Bethune named the facility McLeod Hospital in honor of her parents. The success of McLeod Hospital earned the respect of Negro and white residents. Twenty years after opening, Bethune turned the hospital's equipment over to the municipality.

EMERGING LEADER

The advent of World War I increased the need for Red Cross services. Bethune directed the local Florida chapter of the Red Cross and sponsored a rally on campus attended by U.S. vice president Thomas R. Marshall, Florida governor Sidney J. Cotts, Howard University secretary-treasurer Emmet J. Scott and a host of Washington officials. Holt writes, "This was the first contact the people of Daytona had ever had with a ranking member of their own government...The presence of the vice president was significant for the entire area, but it had a special meaning for Negroes. The fact that he was there through Mrs. Bethune's instrumentality provided her with added leverage." Her leadership skills were helpful in 1928 when a hurricane ravaged southern Florida, devastating the Everglades. Many workers living in this area were seasonal laborers. They lived in tents and shacks and suffered great losses. Many lost their lives, and the majority of homes were demolished. "The wretched hovels in the bog land had been swept away, but parts of the towns were still standing. Workers of all kinds and classes went from door to door pulling down the rafters of buildings that had been devastated by wind." The aftermath of the storm utilized Bethune's campus, as well as churches and public buildings, to house the displaced. Bethune's campus suffered minor damage. She credited God with keeping the campus safe and utilized the situation to continue her fundraising endeavors.

In the second decade of the school's existence, Bethune sought to preserve her school as a private institution. This meant locating dedicated funds from an established source. She turned to the Christian community. A product of Presbyterian and Quaker investment, Bethune knew that many Christian denominations considered education a missionary goal resulting in better citizens. First she approached the Presbyterian Church's Board of Missions for Freedmen. After consideration, the board denied her petition. The Roman Catholic Church offered support, provided that the school become a Catholic institution. This conflicted with her desire to remain non-denominational. The Episcopal Church was suggested by several women on her advisory board. Three members of the trustee board and Gamble, her loyal supporter, were Methodist, so Bethune considered the Methodist Church. Dr. G. Garland Penn, executive secretary of the board of education of the Methodist Church in charge of Negro schools, suggested that Bethune consider merging her institute with Cookman Institute. Cookman was founded in 1872 and was the first school for Negro boys. The merger occurred in 1923. Bethune's school became Bethune-Cookman Collegiate Institute. She voiced her initial displeasure, saying that it was "a big thing to yield all." Yet she concluded that with God's blessing and protection, the work would continue. The Methodist financial backing alleviated a heavy burden, and subsequently, she was left to direct the school once she no longer had to focus so heavily on fundraising. For more than thirty years, through the Great Depression and World War II, she served as the first president and president emeritus, growing the campus property, curriculum and student body.

In 1927, Bethune traveled to Europe for a four-month excursion. Her travel was principally pleasure and some business on behalf of the NACW. She met Lady Nancy Astor, who opened her home to Bethune via a garden party. Bethune toured London, Scotland, Glasgow, Paris, Luxembourg, Belgium, Switzerland and Italy. The global struggle for human rights became clearer for her in Europe after visiting historic locations. As Holt explained, "She realized that the constant struggle of man for freedom, which was in essence the history of man himself, did have a direct bearing upon her own life. She was a direct descendant of this struggle for freedom, and its story was an essential part of her." She prayed that through her own life and testimony, a kinship in the oneness of man would become part of her life's mission. Her travel was free from racial segregation. In London, she was treated with cordiality equal to other visitors. While in Paris, she absorbed a sense of fashion. Her fondness for jewelry meant that she adorned her hands with rings and neck with pearls on a daily basis. When in Berne, Switzerland, she visited the International Garden. Crafted by technicians, the garden held many unique hybrids. A black rose grew in the midst of other roses. Its velvety ebony beauty was no greater or less than other roses. Bethune likened the variety of colors to the hues of man with God as the master gardener. God created skin tone and did not esteem one over the other as each contributed to the beauty of the entire garden. "This sameness of opportunity was all that was asked by humankind of all the races and nations on earth—not to be relegated to one side, but to [grow] and flourish side by side, to completion." She returned home reenergized for service to Negro women. She would describe the progress of women in other countries and remind Negro women to not grow weary in advocating for equality; persistency would benefit their endeavors.

LEADERSHIP IN NACW

The NACW was a collective response to the demands on community resources and the growing racism of the 1890s. Negro women of the Progressive Era forged a national organization dedicated to racial improvement. Local, regional, civic, literary and church groups came together in 1896, resulting in the NACW. The leading members of NACW were educated, notable women whose pedigrees included pre–Civil War free ancestry. The strongest branches were in the northeastern states. The women promoted honesty, justice and protection of Negro women. The violence in southern states precluded NACW from meeting in the south. In 1920 and 1922, the organization held its biennial meetings in Tuskegee and Richmond. During her presidency, Bethune attempted to move the meeting location around the country to remain non-partisan in the regional squabbles brewing among the various women.

Bethune served as the president of the State Federation of Colored Women's Clubs. In 1924, she was elected national president of NACW, a position she held until 1928. During her presidency, Bethune and NACW crusaded for appropriate housing for delinquent Negro girls. Prior to 1924, juvenile Negro girls were housed in adult jails while white juvenile offenders had a facility solely for girls. Bethune secured a defunct jail in Ocala, as well as a matron to maintain the facility. NACW members cleaned the facility and located furniture, while Bethune found funding for operational expenses. The facility served as a classroom, providing the girls with training, guidance and protection. Bethune implored NACW members to recognize discrimination and miseducation as a threat to citizenship. Thus, the women needed to secure proper education for *all* Negro people, ensuring the dismantling of segregation and lack in the community.

Will W. Alexander, a Methodist minister who worked with the YMCA, initiated the Commission on Interracial Cooperation. The first meeting included white and Negro men. The success of the suffrage movement led the men to realize that women held a unique perspective in dealing with discrimination. The suffrage movement was not without its racial problems, however; black and white women organized separately but advocated collectively for the right to vote. The 1924 NACW meeting served as an interracial session where whites and Negroes met. The Negro women voiced their concerns about public safety and education, concerns shared by the white women. The success of the initial meeting resulted in the formation of the Commission on Interracial Cooperation, of which Bethune served as

Front row, left to right: Margaret Murray Washington, Mary McLeod Bethune, Lucy Laney. *Second row, left to right:* unknown, unknown, Charlotte Hawkins Brown and Lugenia Hope Burns. *Courtesy of Moreland Spingarn Research Center Prints and Photographs Division.*

vice-president. Bethune's presidency of the NACW resulted in an invitation to the National Council of Women of the United States in New York being hosted by Eleanor Roosevelt. The National Council of Women was an organization composed of independent organizations that concerned themselves with the opportunities and conditions of women—principally white women.

MEETING THE ROOSEVELT WOMEN

The National Council of Women of the United States enjoyed a luncheon sponsored by Mrs. Eleanor Roosevelt, wife of New York governor Franklin

D. Roosevelt, and Bethune attended as the NACW representative. Nonplussed with being the only black woman in the room, Bethune's trepidation came from being ignored by the majority of white women. A kind gesture from Governor Roosevelt's mother, Sara, who assuredly approached her, took her arm and walked her to the head table, left an indelible impression on Bethune. The impression led to conversations and additional meetings, resulting in a life-long friendship between Bethune and the Roosevelt women. Eleanor Roosevelt accepted an honorary chairmanship of the Bethune-Cookman College endowment campaign. Holt wrote, "Their deep and fundamental common purposes and generous hearts made for an enduring bond which was terminated only by the death of Mrs. Bethune."

Eleanor Roosevelt was more than the wife of New York governor Franklin D. Roosevelt; she herself was an activist. In "Woman of the Century," Blanche Wiesen Cook wrote, "Her journey to greatness, her voyage out beyond the confines of good wife and devoted mother, involved determination and amazing courage. It also involved one of history's most unique partnerships. [FDR] admired his wife, appreciated her strengths and depended on her integrity." Roosevelt's compassion, advocacy and liberalism stretched the position of First Lady beyond then known limits. Born Anna Eleanor Roosevelt in October 1884 and nine years Bethune's junior, she grew up in a racially divided America. Her personal life was marked with tragedy when she was orphaned in 1892. Mary Hall, her maternal grandmother, gained custody of her and her siblings. Roosevelt, like Bethune, was deemed physically unattractive and, at times, homely. Nevertheless, neither woman believed themselves ugly for being less than industry-standard beauties. Roosevelt wrote, "I was a solemn child without beauty. I seemed like a little old woman entirely lacking in the spontaneous joy and mirth of youth."

Like Bethune, Roosevelt found liberation in education under the instructive hand of a special teacher. Mademoiselle Marie Souvestre of the Allenswood Academy in London imbued her with a sense of mission and purpose. Souvestre presented herself as an articulate woman committed to liberal causes. Moreover, her political leanings, passion for history and enthusiastic approach to issues shaped Roosevelt's social consciousness and political development. Roosevelt recalled the years at Allenswood as the happiest of her life. The strength of Souvestre contributed to her own confidence and sense of purpose.

Roosevelt returned to her America in 1902, rejoining her siblings. Her private passion for political involvement morphed into appeasing her family's position on social responsibility. She joined the National Consumers League as well as the Promotion of Settlement Movements junior division. Her social and civic work contributed to her sense of value, and her filial duty led to her meeting her future husband, Franklin D. Roosevelt. The two Roosevelts were distant cousins and attracted to one another. Their sixteenth-month courtship resulted in a March 1905 marriage, to the disapproval of FDR's mother, Sara Roosevelt. Their love for each other and their interest in larger social issues kept the two committed to the marriage of ideas while the nuptial relationship ebbed and flowed with extra-marital issues, staunch ideological differences and general peccadilloes. Yet they remained married. The relationship produced six children, two presidential administrations and a kind yet overbearing mother-in-law.

FDR's rise in politics moved Roosevelt away from her mother-in-law and into a space and place of freedom. His political career and her spousal responsibility contributed to her understanding of her personal and political identities. World War I offered her additional space to craft her personal identity as well as to escape the emotional and petty rollercoaster of political wives' circles. She became consumed with wartime work where she dedicated time to the Navy Relief and the Red Cross canteen. The work contributed to a sense of purpose and a realization that she could move in a sphere of personal interests, not solely to advance the career of her husband. The newfound fulfillment occupied her time with visits to hospitals and government facilities. When asked to visit shell-shocked servicemen in Washington's Saint Elizabeth's Hospital, the poor conditions she witnessed there resulted in her urging Secretary of the Interior Franklin Lane to visit the facility. Lane declined, but Roosevelt pushed until he appointed a commission to investigate supply shortages and general conditions. She wrote in her memoirs, "I became more determined to try for certain ultimate objectives. I had gained a certain assurance as to my ability to run things, and the knowledge that there is joy in accomplishing good."

During the 1920s, she realized that her increasing political expertise and new support system was an outgrowth of her husband's network. She sought to maintain a duality with her newfound political space. She invested her time in the Democratic Women's Committee (DWC), the Todhunter School for Girls and Val-Kill, which lay outside Albany. Val-Kill was a former factory that she converted into a fairly comfortable house, retreat and office for her secretary Malvina Thompson. These extracurricular activities allowed her more independence as well as efficiently dividing her life between being governor's wife and mother/citizen.

In March 1933, Roosevelt entered the White House with apprehension over her new position as first lady. At the same time, she was forty-eight years old, had taught school, raised a family, managed a business and engaged in social/political issues. Her increasing consciousness was mature and ripe to address national and international issues. The visibility and restrictions on her movements were daunting. However, before she left the White House in 1941, she radically changed the possibilities for future first ladies. She held her own press conference and announced that she would meet with female reporters once a week. Like Bethune, she realized the power of the pen and published a newspaper column titled "My Day." One biographer stated that Roosevelt left a paper trail over six miles long. Her long-term goal with the press was to attain respect and achieve cooperation. Through her press conferences, she wanted the general public to know the workings of the government, especially White House activities, and provide opportunities for female journalists.

During the course of the Depression, Roosevelt was involved in establishing the National Youth Administration (NYA). Historians argue about the extent to which she was involved, but her influence is evident in the agency's development. The NYA was created by an executive order signed by FDR on June 26, 1935, and it sought to administer programs in five areas: work projects, vocational guidance, apprenticeship training, life skills guidance camps for unemployed women and student financial aid for college students. Roosevelt was the logical person to oversee the agency in light of her earlier political work. She connected with agency directors and arranged meetings with officials, youth leaders and interested parties to meet with President Roosevelt. She conducted visits to the over one hundred NYA sites.

Through the NYA and the NCNW, Roosevelt and Bethune crafted the National Conference of Negro Women at the White House in 1938. In February 1939, she resigned from the Daughters of the American Revolution, the owners of Constitution Hall, because the DAR refused to rent the auditorium to black contralto Marian Anderson. Roosevelt used her newspaper column to disgrace the DAR and would later lend her support in 1949 when coloratura soprano Carol Brice was also denied use of the Constitution Hall because of a whites-only clause in its lease. She embraced the Double V campaign waged by black Americans, which sought victory over fascism in Europe and segregation in America. Roosevelt argued that American racism was equivalent to fascism, saying that if one and not the other were left unaddressed, it would be hypocritical.

First Lady Eleanor Roosevelt at the dedication of the Council House. Mrs. Roosevelt, a friend of Mrs. Bethune, gave comments and attended the public ceremony in support of NCNW. *Courtesy Mary McLeod Bethune Council House, NPS.*

Bethune and Roosevelt shared similar interests concerning women and equal rights. Separated along racial and regional lines, as well as nearly ten years in age, the two women's larger concerns evolved into a lifelong friendship. Roosevelt's radical approach to social and political issues provided Bethune and the NCNW an audience with President Roosevelt. Their friendship afforded NCNW with an annual White House meeting and Bethune with a federal appointment.

CHAPTER 2

Becoming a Washington Resident

Washington is a unique city. There is the federal government and the
local community. The local community is composed of more than
120 neighborhoods with distinct histories and culture within four quadrants:
northwest, northeast, southwest and southeast. Unfortunately there is no
official neighborhood listing for Washington, except for historic districts.
The number is fluid and constantly changing. The principal location of
governmental and educational activity is in the northwest quadrant, which
contains the White House, five major universities, local government offices
and a host of embassies. The northeast area hosts government agencies, the
Library of Congress, the Supreme Court and Union Station. Southwest is
principally the waterfront and contains numerous churches and residential
housing. The southeastern area houses the St. Elizabeth Hospital, as well as
residential housing.

In the early twentieth century, racial segregation was the norm. Basically
an upper southern city, Washington neighborhoods were stratified along
racial and class lines. The poorer communities were checkerboard blocks
of black and white residents. Many residents accepted their living situations
while attending segregated churches, schools and movie theaters. There
were racial scuffles between blacks and whites and struggles between police
officers and citizens, as well as red-lining by real estate agents.

Black Washington was segregated from white Washington and largely
segmented into various pools within black society. The lines of division
placed blacks into categories of pedigreed natives, neo-natives, middle

class, poor, educated and uneducated, fair and dark complexioned, home owners and alley dwellers. The complex social matrix of black society has roots in the nineteenth century, when social norms became an unwritten yet understood social hierarchy. The aristocratic nature of black Washington is attributed to the nature of enslavement and being the first freed. The enslavement system in Washington allowed many to cultivate their skills and earn their freedom through self-purchase. Concurrently, President Lincoln's compensated emancipation trial in 1862 liberated three thousand enslaved persons. The former enslavers were compensated $300 per person, while the enslaved person was offered $100 to relocate to Liberia or Haiti. Many chose to remain in Washington in light of their skills and entrepreneurial opportunities. Conversely, the opportunities for improvement grew for some and not for others. Poverty from the increased number of black residents after the Civil War resulted in people living where they could. The effort to survive developed into alley dwellings, housing behind proper housing. In *The Paper Bag Principle Class, Colorism, and Rumor and the Case of Black Washington, D.C.*, Audrey Elisa Kerr writes, "What is more, the alley system resulted in the complete and total isolation of poor blacks." The physical and social isolation contributed to stereotyping within the black community. Kerr explains:

> *Three distinct social classes and living areas emerged in the city. A handful of wealthy blacks owned homes in the southeastern part of the District. Middle-class blacks, most of whom were employed as government clerks, formed a "second rank," residing along Sixteenth Street between Scott Avenue and the White House. This broad and well-paved avenue running through the heart of the city was closed to the "third rank," the poor black majority, who continued to live east of the Capitol.*

Black Washington entered the twentieth century with an increasing number of migrants from the south. The new arrivals sought government jobs and public school opportunities and brought new customs and practices. By the 1920s, well-to-do black Washington embraced education and W.E.B. DuBois's Talented Tenth ideology. DuBois believed that the educated elite would rescue the race and provide leadership. In the 1930s, Washington welcomed Bethune, and other New Dealers brought to aid the federal government.

PRESIDENT ROOSEVELT CALLS:
NATIONAL YOUTH ADMINISTRATION

Bethune increased her political connections beyond Eleanor Roosevelt throughout the 1930s. She served on the American Child Health Association (ACHA). Her ACHA work involved designing national surveys on infant mortality and public health programs. The results were astounding and led to a campaign to improve training and supplies for women and children. In 1935, the ACHA disbanded. Bethune was a registered Republican who supported FDR's administration. The Coolidge and Hoover administrations' indifference toward black social issues drove many to support the Democrats. The "lily-white" attitude of the Republicans in the south and numerous other affronts resulted in Bethune referring to herself as a New Dealer. FDR's "willingness to appoint racial liberals to key government posts encouraged African Americans" according to Joyce A. Hanson.

In 1934, President Roosevelt issued Executive Order No. 7086 inaugurating the National Youth Administration under the direction of Aubrey Williams. The NYA sought "to prevent human erosion" among American youth. Williams was a college-educated Alabaman and racial liberal who fought during World War I. After the war, he entered into public service with the Federal Emergency Relief Administration. In 1934, he was appointed to the WPA and served the NYA. Williams suggested that the NYA have two black appointees. The first was Mordecai Johnson, president of Howard University. The second was Bethune.

The NYA sought to engage youth ages sixteen to twenty-five through vocational training, scholarships and job placement. The investment in the youth provided future generations with practical skills. Of the 21 million youth, nearly 7 million were out of school, unemployed or on relief. The numbers for black youth in need were double those of whites. In *Mary McLeod Bethune and the National Council of Negro Women: Pursuing a True and Unfettered Democracy*, Elaine M. Smith writes, "With unprecedented and staggering unemployment during the middle of the Great Depression, youth deserved special attention because they constituted about one-third of all the unemployment and they lacked work experience and work habits vis-à-vis other workers." The depressed economy hit black Americans extremely hard as they lost jobs to white people. There were multiple examples where racial discrimination favored white people with regard to federal government–aided relief. Black farmers and domestic workers experienced economic hardships prior to Bethune's appointment, but her position directed relief aid.

Mary M. Bethune at President Roosevelt's inauguration in 1934. *Courtesy Mary McLeod Bethune Council House, NPS.*

In June 1935, FDR considered Bethune for a federal appointment after she was awarded the Spingarn Medal. The Spingarn Medal is the NAACP's highest honor, which Bethune received for her race work and commitment to social justice. Bethune remarked that self-help and responsibility were keys to overcoming discrimination. Josephine Roche, assistant secretary of the Treasury, presented Bethune's award. Roche also served on the NYA's committee. After hearing the acceptance speech, she believed that Bethune deserved a position within the NYA. Roosevelt and Roche discussed Bethune, and both agreed. Within six weeks after receiving the award, Bethune personally met with Roosevelt, who asked her to become a member of the NYA advisory committee. She accepted. Once involved, she expanded her limited role. The needs of black people were dire, and the opportunities for black youth to improve themselves aided the larger black community. Bethune stated, "Through the program of the [NYA] touching the humblest black boy of the South has come to the realization on the part of thousands of untutored Negro parents that the government does care."

In 1936, her first report impressed FDR. She was then appointed head of the Office of Minority Affairs in NYA. She used the appointment to assist black students on predominantly black college campuses. She viewed the federal appointment as a tri-fold benefit. She ensured that blacks received their fair share, opened federal positions for other blacks and advocated for black women. Bethune worked within the segregated government, and, as Hanson describes, "she outwardly accepted the inevitability of racial separation as long as [blacks] had power over separate programs." As director, she appointed fourteen blacks to state NYA committees. By 1939, she had increased the state administrators to twenty-six, six of whom were women. She selected who would move forward and when. She visited every state where blacks worked on behalf of the NYA. Hanson states, "The controlling aspect of her personality is readily apparent in the way she ran the Office of Minority Affairs."

In 1940, she understood her political capital. The election afforded her leverage with Democrats on behalf of the black vote. Her organizational influence within the NAACP, Urban League and NCNW elevated her from educator to self-appointed politician and race representative. She made it known that she was not a puppet of FDR's administration, nor was she in agreement with all of his policies. She selected times to voice her displeasure. Her autonomy resulted in her joining the National Negro Congress (NNC). The NNC's first meeting in 1936 called for unity of action among the 585 organizations in attendance. The vision of organizational unity clicked with her, but the diversity of the involved organizations challenged effectiveness. NNC president John Davis wrote Bethune about hosting a Negro Youth event, and Bethune assumed control. With assistance from Roosevelt, the NNC youth report was known to all federal officials. Appreciative of the progress made, black youth still suffered inequality. Bethune hosted a follow-up conference under the auspices of NYA, and FDR attended. Bethune employed her position to air grievances and acquired positions for black youth.

As a Washington resident, she participated in local protests, like the New Negro Alliance (NNA) picket lines against People's Drugstore. People's operated forty-four stores in predominately black neighborhoods but did

not proportionally hire black workers. The NNA was a successful protest movement that utilized economic weapons in the fight for civil rights. William Hastie, a native of Tennessee raised in Washington, was an early member of the NNA. Hastie, a Harvard graduate and assistant solicitor in the Interior Department, understood the link between protest and policy change. Bethune also participated in the protests against the DAR's refusal to let Marian Anderson sing in Constitution Hall. She was instrumental in involving Roosevelt in the protest. She did not know that the groundwork for protesting against the DAR would help ten years later when the same issue arose in response to a performance by Carol Brice.

In 1939, she organized the Federal Council of Negro Affairs, commonly known as the Black Cabinet. Coalition and unity were central to Bethune, and the Black Cabinet included representatives from every major department. Bethune also utilized race leaders outside of the government from Howard and organizational contacts. Bethune often stated, "We are here to think together. Let us not lose sight of our objective; what these committees are after is a larger participation of Negroes in the upper brackets of government."

Bethune continued to push for the inclusion of black women within the government. The wall of segregation chipped and cracked but did not crumble. She fell short of her ultimate goal of universal acceptance of black women on the strength of their education and ability, without the impediments of race and gender. She believed that education and skills benefitted the workplace regardless of the worker's gender or racial identity and that discrimination was a disservice to American society. Meanwhile, conservatives chipped away at the NYA, resulting its closure in 1943. The Senate approved a hefty budget of $50 million, but the House allocated nothing. The denied appropriation resulted in the liquidation of NYA funds. Smith wrote, "Congressional Republicans, however, killed it. They were motivated by 'race mixing' on many projects, equal benefits to blacks, primarily in the last year, [and] the votes that it might generate for the Democratic nominee in the next presidential election."

Opposite: Mrs. William Hastie and Mary McLeod Bethune are seen protesting on Fourteen and U Streets, Northwest. *Courtesy Moorland Spingarn Research Center Prints and Photographs Division.*

The closure of the NYA saddened Bethune, especially in light of the lost opportunities for American youth. It took one year for NYA operations to close. During this time, she was without a job and in need of a new place to live. Eleanor Roosevelt approached FDR to locate a new position for Bethune. They found one in the War Department. In providing testimonial for Bethune, FDR wrote, "As a woman and as a Negro she has been effectively concerned for a better chance for all Americans and better training to meet the widening opportunities…in honoring her, not merely as leader of women and a leader of her race, but as an American."

Bethune employed the NCNW in opening the doors for black women. Many skilled women, black and white, flooded into Washington answering the report to service. However, when top jobs were open, federal employers almost always selected white women. The black women were also overlooked when seeking housing. Dorothy Height recalled, "[Mrs. Day] said I should know that Washington was deeply divided between the masses and the classes…I had to think twice about where I would live in Washington, she said, because if I lived among the masses, I would never be accepted by the classes…when I moved to Washington that fall of 1939, the city was completely segregated. There was not a toilet downtown that a black person could use. Union Station was the only place a black person could get a sandwich." Bethune, now autonomous and familiar with Washington, used the next six years to fully engage in activism and education on behalf of Negro girls and women nationally and internationally.

SHOWCASING NEGRO WOMEN: NCNW AT 1318 VERMONT AVENUE, NORTHWEST

Bethune was active during the 1930s. She administered her school in Daytona, served on NACW's committees, accepted a federal appointment with the NYA and founded the NCNW. The formation of the NCNW inaugurated the second half of her life. All of her efforts and training culminated in and benefitted NCNW. The 1930s was a decade of immense poverty and lack, which further motivated Bethune to provide for black women by ensuring that there was a clearinghouse established to locate needs and find funding to aid rural, southern and overlooked communities. NCNW would not be another organization but a coalition of organizations, the expertise of which vocalized local, regional and constituency groups on issues concerning black women. The national impact of the Depression quickened in Bethune the need for a national clearinghouse for black women.

The entrenched segregation directed New Deal relief along racial lines within specific regions. A national black women's organization with national influence could sway the balance of provisions afforded black people. Hanson wrote, "Bethune saw racism as a national problem…She concluded that [blacks] must join forces with people of color worldwide while fighting for integration within American society."

However, Bethune realized that the staid methods of the NACW did not consider the detrimental effects of classism on black people; thus 1935 seemed an auspicious time to craft another organization. NACW's foundation was righteous, but its methods pandered to classist notions about poverty being a mindset needing better examples and not a cause of economic injustice. Bethune recognized the links between segregation and poverty from working in the NYA. According to Hanson, "She argued that conditions for [blacks] would not improve simply because of the personal habits of a certain group… She insisted that fundamental changes in American social, economic, and political structure were necessary for racial progress." Bethune envisioned her National Council as a union of educational, business, religious, fraternal and welfare associations under one umbrella. The collective would benefit from the strength of individual organizations all advocating for the Negro woman. The organization would provide educational opportunities, encourage political action and train and hone women's leadership skills. "Bethune [believed] in the moral superiority of women and their primary responsibility for sustaining the ethical strength of the race…She [believed] in the principle of socially responsible individualism, trusting that women would use public positions for group advancement…[She] envisioned this new organization as a vehicle for realizing equality for *all* African Americans."

In New York on December 5, 1935, Bethune called together leadership of fourteen women's organizations. She discussed the urgent need to broaden the work of their respective groups and unite their total strength in joint action on behalf of Negro women. Her proposed organization did not seek to dilute the individual character of any one group. The majority enthusiastically voted to become a permanent organization named the National Council of Negro Women.

Born in the dreary and tumultuous mid-thirties, its struggle for existence paralleled the struggle which the nation was passing through. The lamps of civilization that were slowly but steadily being extinguished in many parts of the world, the frightening and continuous global crises that finally impaled the entire world in war, caught the Council up in the vortex as indeed everything else was and the finality of purpose of the [NCNW] was definitely chartered by the gravity of the time. The [NCNW] therefore was the seed from which growth and integration was to come and by virtue of its national character, activities would be carried out on a national level.

Some questioned the intentions of another organization whose future could mimic the foibles of earlier groups. Charlotte Hawkins Brown, founder and principal of Palmer Memorial Institute in Sedalia, North Carolina, thought the idea too lofty. Mary Church Terrell, founder and inaugural president of NACW, cautiously endorsed Bethune's vision. On April 29, 1936, in Sojourner Truth Hall on Howard's campus, the NCNW met to adopt its constitution and elect permanent officers. The slate read:

> *President—Mrs. Mary McLeod Bethune*
> *First Vice President—Dr. Charlotte Hawkins Brown*
> *Second Vice President—Mrs. Christine Smith*
> *Third Vice President—Dr. Eudora Ashburn*
> *Fourth Vice President—Mrs. Mary Church Terrell*
> *Recording Secretary—Mrs. Florence K. Williamson*
> *Executive Secretary—Dean Lucy D. Slowe*
> *Treasurer—Mrs. Addie W. Dickerson*

On July 25, 1936, the NCNW was incorporated in Washington. The principal business address was Dean Slowe's campus office. The certificate of incorporation adopted four purposes for the organization: to unite national member organizations into the NCNW; to educate, encourage and effect the participation of Negro women in civic, political, economic and educational activities and institutions; to serve as a clearinghouse for the dissemination of activities concerning women; and to plan, initiate and carry out projects that develop, benefit and integrate the Negro and the nation. The purposes were dynamic elements of the NCNW that would enlarge according to the needs of the time. The initial headquarters was Bethune's living room, and funds were raised from yearly member organization assessments of $50.00. The national program was executed by thirteen committees assigned to particular interests ranging from public affairs to employment to rural life to types of membership.

During its infancy, NCNW's programs advocated for black women while collecting, publishing and disseminating facts about Negro women's lives in America. Employment and postwar opportunities impelled NCNW to scrutinize the federal and private sectors. To combat segregation, it offered job training and counseling to provide women with skills needed to secure employment. The workshops focused on skills, dress, conversation and patriotism, precluding any obvious reason for denying a well-trained woman a job. The war effort provided an international stage for Negro women to show themselves able.

> *The* [NCNW] *took a decisive and leading role in the campaigns pertaining to the Negro in the military. The Council advocated integration of Negroes into all branches of the military and worked for the admission of women into the WACS and the Waves along with other organizations.* [NCNW] *inspected camps where Negro women were trained and discussed complaints and charges brought by civilians and military persons pertaining to conditions which they felt were unjust and unfair....Numerous campaigns in support of the government and their efforts to meet certain national problems were projected by* [NCNW] *and these events included* [We Serve America and Hold Your Job, all] *implemented by* [most] *local councils enthusiastically.*

Lastly, NCNW utilized the black press and media outlets to foster better race relations. Bethune was a master spokeswoman and believed her deportment, speech and knowledge served as a living example of the potential of the Negro woman. NCNW published its own journal and newsletter for its membership and archives, both documenting past and present accomplishments.

The overall structure of NCNW reflected a shift within the black women's club movement. Unlike earlier groups, the NCNW sought to attract membership from Negro women's organizations as well as individuals. The organizations were not solely collegiate or professional groups; they also included religious, masonic and neighborhood/regional clubs. She welcomed grassroots organizations whose purpose served the larger black community. Hanson wrote, "Local activists were capable of organizing individual actions; [the structure] of NCNW was designed to incorporate community activists into a wider program focused on national legislative reform [all] concentrated on empowering women by helping them find ways to achieve economic independence [to bring] about long-term political change." Bethune's NCNW would "take off their hats, leave mink coats back and roll up their sleeves ready for work." She cherished the poor country girl that she had been, but opportunity afforded her entry into bourgeois habits. Scheduled hair appointments, facials and fine clothing warred with her desire to remain totally connected to her humble beginnings. Moreover, she was aware that black society never fully embraced her. Toward this end, she took absolute control of NCNW and directed the organization from a regal, inclusive and austere perch, positioning herself as a personal of influence.

The NCNW chipped away at segregation through living above the fray. Workshops, conferences, articles, journals, awards ceremonies and invitations extended to international leaders positioned NCNW as a viable solution to discrimination through equipping black women. From 1935 to 1940, NCNW grew, adding affiliates growing from ten to nearly twenty organizations. As early as 1940, Bethune seeded the idea of a national headquarters for NCNW. By 1943, Bethune's NYA was closed, NCNW was growing and her living room was an inconvenient place to operate a national organization. Smith wrote, "No organization with about a score of national affiliates, dozens of local chapters, and hundreds of life members could hope to function effectively without a business-like headquarters." The NCNW leadership endorsed her idea. The 1940 minutes state that the headquarters "shall be a memorial and shrine in honor of those pioneer Negro women leaders who hewed a pathway for us to follow." The group desired its headquarters to be a permanent meeting place open to community groups and reflective of black women's thrift.

Bethune's search for a property had to meet requirements befitting her influence and NCNW's rising prominence. The row house on Vermont Avenue suited her desire. Bethune collected the initial down payment of $500. Through her friend Eleanor Roosevelt, Bethune approached Marshall Field, a wealthy Chicago businessman who listened to Bethune's request and provided her with a check for $10,000. The generous donation from Field allowed NCNW to move in. NCNW purchased the house for $15,000.

The property on Vermont Avenue appealed to Bethune for a variety of reasons. She probably visualized the space as small but adequate for office and residential space. The dining room would serve as a boardroom while the upper level would be bedrooms for visitors or roomers. Another desirable feature was the interracial neighborhood of working-class and professional people. It was also within a five-block walking distance of the White House and numerous Negro places, such as Woodson's Association for the Study of Negro Life and History offices and the Phyllis Wheatley YWCA, the oldest

Negro branch in the city, as well as historic Vermont Avenue Baptist Church and Baptist Training Seminary.

The history of the building begins with the occupancy of John J. McElhone, who worked for the House of Representatives in various capacities. In the 1880 census, the McElhone family included his wife, three minor-age children and three female servants, two black and one white. In 1890, the property was valued at $7,000. The census listed three working male adults: father, John J., stenographer; son James F, a clerk; and Phillip, a reporter. John died in June 1890. His widow, Mary, inherited the property but sold it to reduce her debts. Put up for auction, the house fetched $14,600, which was $100 more than what Mary needed to pay off her debts.

The second occupant of the property was Frank G. Carpenter. Carpenter was a newspaper correspondent and known writer. In the 1900 census, his family consisted of a wife, two children and two live-in black female servants. The Carpenter family occupied the house until 1911. The house was sold in the winter of 1912 to Alphonso and Anna Gravalles. Alphonso was self-employed as the owner of a tailoring shop. He specialized in women's apparel fashionable for the era. The Gravalles family occupied the house longest. They lived in 1318 for over thirty years. During their tenure, they modified the property, adding a carriage house and porch in the backyard. The 1930 census listed the occupants as two Gravalles daughters, a niece and a boarder.

The Logan Circle neighborhood experienced change during the residency of the first three owners.

> *Although much of the early development in the Logan Circle area consisted of middle and lower class dwellings, by 1892…the area had emerged as one of the most diverse socio-economic areas of the city that catered to all levels of society. Over the years, as the city center grew increasingly dense and transportation improved, white residents with the means to do so relocated into the new "suburban" developments in the higher elevations of the city, and although Logan Circle itself and the enclave on Vermont Avenue south of the Circle remained largely white into the 1930s…The shift in the racial composition of the Logan Circle area occurred gradually, beginning in 1900, and it would take another twenty years for the number of black residents to noticeably increase.*

On April 4, 1930, Iowa Circle became Logan Circle. The name change was initiated by Congressman Arthur Capper. He introduced HR7996 to

Congress to acknowledge the accomplishments of John Alexander Logan, a Civil War veteran, lawyer, politician and resident of Iowa Circle at number 4. Logan Circle consists of a center circle with six spokes, three northwest and three southeast. The streets were P Street, Rhode Island Avenue, Vermont Avenue and Thirteenth Street. The physical circle is ringed with row houses occupied by notable residents and professional and accomplished people. Attorneys Belford and Marjorie Lawson lived at 8 Logan Circle. Holiness preacher Emanuel "Sweet Daddy" Grace lived at 11 Logan Circle. Heavyweight boxing champion Jack Johnson lived in Logan Circle in the 1920s, while a number of black car dealerships occupied Fourteenth Street, along with segregated fire station #4.

On December 18, 1943, NCNW leadership and its legal committee consented to the purchase. According to Smith:

> *Collectively, these twenty-four women constituted a driving force... Attorney Sadie Alexander exclaimed that the place was "beyond our comprehension"...Moreover, they voted that their beloved President [have] the right to live in the house for life, free of charge. Even so, Bethune probably wound up paying for her quarters, one way or another. It would be her Washington residence until confidant Sadie Franklin packed up her things on November 21, 1950.*

Bethune sought the assistance of individuals in upgrading the property and furnishing the rooms. NCNW affiliates and private citizens contributed. Congressman William L. Dawson donated a mahogany conference table and chairs. Alpha Kappa Alpha outfitted the NCNW offices while Delta Sigma Theta decorated soror Bethune's office. Madame C.J. Walker donated Bethune's bedroom and dressing room furnishings. Emma Kelley, founder of the Daughters of Elks women's society affiliated with the Improved Benevolent Protective Order of Elks of the World, was honored by a front bedroom donated by her daughter Buena Kelly. Audley Moore furnished the third bedroom in memory of Bessye Bearden, former NCNW treasurer. The International Workers Order contributed $1,000 to the work of the council. Bethune pledged to use the funds to set up an international room, "a room that will be cultural and beautiful where women of all races may feel free to come and rest and commune with us. We have found it so difficult for women of certain types to find a place for overnight in the various hotels because of race or color. Our international room will welcome women of all races and colors." The renovations and outfitting of the property took nearly a year. Once everything was in place, NCNW dedicated the building on October 15, 1944.

The program was held in front of the property. At 4:00 p.m., excerpts of Dvorak's symphony *From the New World* played. The Lord's Prayer was read, and Bethune welcomed everyone. Bethune stated, "This house has been obtained by the prayers and sacrifice of a few, but the devotion, idealism and ambition which surround it will spread to many; and the inspired efforts which it shall generate in years to come will be felt around the world." In attendance was educator Charlotte Hawkins Brown, First Lady Eleanor Roosevelt, social worker Agnes Meyer, NCNW house committee chairman Dorothy Ferebee and Pastor Robert M. Williams of historic Asbury Methodist Episcopal Church. Brown commented:

> *It represents not only the gifts of the intelligentsia who have enjoyed unusual privileges and achieved noble successes in public endeavors, but the nickels and dimes from the rank and file of Negro women whose love and confidence in this movement and its leader have no bounds. At a time when women all over the world are being aroused to assume grave responsibilities in regard to our present situation as contenders for freedom, it is not only meet, but absolutely necessary that the women of America's largest minority group should pool their resources and gather what strength they may to take their well-earned places by the side of women of all other races in our civilized world...It stands for unity of purpose and ideals; it is an open sesame to united endeavors to prove to the world that Negro womanhood can go forward to battle against the evils and handicaps that beset the paths of all women not withstanding their struggle for the enjoyment of rights and privileges vouchsafed to the womanhood of all other races and denied to them. Here we can meet and so plan and direct our thinking in channels of service to our country in its post war plans, rehabilitating the gallant lads of all races who will be returned to us...Let [it] not be said that we dedicate this building to Negro womanhood alone, for if democracy is to be a reality in our beloved America, white women, black women, red women, yellow women must find their way through these doors and in consultation, meditation and prayer approach world problems under the guidance of Almighty God.*

The affiliates participated in the dedication. Chi Eta Phi, a nursing sorority, and Delta Sigma Theta social services held events during the course of the dedication. Esther Shaw's poem "Jewels of Distinction" expresses the

Above: Mrs. Bethune speaks at the dedication ceremony for the council house. Eleanor Roosevelt is seated in the background. *Courtesy Mary McLeod Bethune Council House, NPS.*

Opposite, top: Mrs. Bethune, Dorothy Ferebee and four others are pictured at the dedication of the council house. *Courtesy Mary McLeod Bethune Council House, NPS.*

Opposite, bottom: Mary M. Bethune speaks at the house dedication. *Courtesy Mary McLeod Bethune Council House, NPS.*

Above: Mary McLeod Bethune addresses the audience at the outdoor dedication ceremony for the council house. *Courtesy Mary McLeod Bethune Council House, NPS.*

Opposite, top: Jewels [Chi Eta Phi] at dedication of council house in Washington, DC. *Courtesy Mary McLeod Bethune Council House, NPS.*

Opposite, bottom: Delta Sigma Theta Sorors and guests celebrate the establishment of the national headquarters in Washington, D.C. *From left to right:* Patricia Harris, Dorothy P. Harrison, Mamie Eisenhower, Dorothy Height, Mrs. Reber Cann and Letitia Johnson Lightfoot. *Courtesy Mary McLeod Bethune Council House, NPS.*

resilience of black women, reflected in the diamond's purity, emerald's devotion, garnet's determination, ruby's courage, sapphire's loyalty and onyx's patience.

In the 1944 *Aframerican Journal*, an article entitled "1318 Vermont" described a bit of the property's surroundings for those who were unable to attend the dedication ceremony. "[T]he bronze figure of Martin Luther, looking to the South. In his face is the light of prophecy for all groups who enter upon bold ventures...the Council from its new locality could carry forward a more extensive program of education, concentrating in the field of labor, economics, interracial and international cooperation and citizenship." In the *Chicago Defender* on October 28, 1944, Rebecca Stiles Taylor reported on the house dedication.

Atty Elsie Austin who told the story of the council and the headquarters at the dedication...I am all women in whose veins flows the blood of black men. From my lineage have come prophets and kings, artists and scientists, educators and workers, who have given their contributions to all men and all nations. Great love has made me know the power of the heart—has kept me free from hatred and coldness. With it I have given help and comfort to all mankind...Great vision has forced me to struggle on to what shall bring goodness, truth, justice and unity to civilization. Let it never be said that I desired a better world only for my own people—for I have worked and served and achieved in all the continents of the world for all mankind. To this house I bring my gifts of the mind and spirit that it may find hope, light and guidance to what shall make a nobler world.

PUBLISHING AND PRESERVING NEGRO WOMEN'S HISTORY

Black club women sought to present themselves as respectable, patriotic citizens. This image refuted media-crafted stereotypes. Many derogatory images of black women were throwbacks to enslavement-era plantation scenes depicting the women as ignorant, servile creatures without intelligence. Thus, many black club women, in line with the black press, proudly published their exploits, successes, culture and history to present themselves correctly. Bethune continued in this tradition when NCNW published the *Aframerican Women's Journal* and the *Telefact*. These two publications served the membership and the larger black community to inform, solicit members, celebrate successes of the race and document achievements past and present. The unique nature of each publication was tailor-made for a particular audience. The *Telefact*, created for the membership, provided warm, informative and strategic insight into NCNW affiliates about successful campaigns, membership drives, political issues, national meetings and life matters of general membership. The *Telefact* reads like a series of quarterly reports that shed light on the intimate and semi-informal character of NCNW during its formative years.

Conversely, the *Aframerican Women's Journal* displayed the professional image of the NCNW. The magazine's layout, photographs, letter from the president and roundup of affiliate activities established NCNW as the vanguard women's group preemptively documenting their achievements as well as acknowledging foremothers in the struggle for civil and human rights. The *Aframerican* launched in 1940 under the editorship of Sue Bailey Thurman. Thurman was a dynamo, born August 26, 1903, to Reverend Isaac and Susie Ford Bailey of Pine Bluff, Arkansas, the youngest of ten children. She too came from a large, pious family. She attended Spelman Seminary, and she earned bachelor's degrees in music and liberal arts from Oberlin College in 1926. After completing her education, she became involved in the YWCA, working as national traveling secretary for the YWCA's college division. During her tenure, she lectured in various European countries on behalf of the YWCA. In 1932, she married Dr. Howard Thurman, a theologian and social critic. The Thurmans' innovative love for social justice and philosophical belief in the brotherhood of man allowed their professional careers to become entwined. She came to Washington with her husband in 1932 when he assumed the position of dean of the Chapel at Howard. While in the city, she connected to the NCNW and served as the founder and editor of the *Aframerican Women's Journal* for four years. The *Aframerican Women's Journal* was the first NCNW publication. In later years, the publication changed its name to *Women United*. In the inaugural publication of *Women United*, Bethune wrote:

> *This magazine goes to press just as my work as founder and first president of the National Council of Negro Women, which this publication represents, draws to a close. This is my last issue, but it is to be hoped that many more issues will appear as other fine women take the reins of administration in their capable hands, and carry on the work that the years have compelled me to lay down. Our magazine,* Women United*—which is our official organ—must have your increased support. Its circulation must be greatly extended. We must pass our copies from hand to hand and get new subscribers—new friends. For unless it is better known it cannot grow. We need an "angel" for our magazine who will underwrite its expenses for one, two or three years, while it is becoming established. But until such an angel appears, we must work hard at being our own angels—at making every copy of this magazine do the work of many copies to carry our thinking to the women of America and of the world! I want to take this opportunity to express my gratitude to Sue Bailey Thurman, our first editor, and to those who have followed her, for their efforts to make the* Aframerican Woman's Journal *and the* Women United*, which succeeded, a worthy reflection of the work, objectives and interests of Council membership.*

In the tradition established by Thurman, the NCNW leading magazine published insightful articles about political issues and NCNW activities to address societal matters. Thurman was also instrumental in founding and locating funding for the NCNW library and archives project. A well-traveled, educated and religious woman, her contributions to the publication and archives of the NCNW were invaluable.

Select items in the *Telefact* and the *Aframerican Women's Journal* demonstrate the local/national citizenship of Bethune and NCNW. These two publications were instrumental in the NCNW establishing its presence and position as the chief advocate on behalf of Negro women and children. Moreover, they served as viable archival documents to junior counsel members and generations of black women would could touch and read about the accomplishments of earlier eras. The struggles and strategies employed would empower black women collectively through the actions of Bethune and NCNW women. The *Telefact* lists women by name, region and affiliation, thereby writing into the historical record contributions by all Negro women who contributed to the Council, the race and humanity. Finally, the publications served as a recruiting tool and educational opportunity for visitors to the House. In 1943, the first *Telefact* was published. The membership newsletter debuted the same year of the House purchase. These two events were grand accomplishments for Bethune. Moreover, *Telefact* provided information from a membership perspective about the newly purchased headquarters and the formalization of NCNW. The inaugural issue stated:

> *TELEFACT makes initial appearance. In order to keep Council members in touch with official business of the Council; current national, state and local matters affecting women in particular activities of the various affiliated organizations and individual council members; and to secure your cooperation on special national projects being sponsored by the national office; a monthly bulletin called TELEFACT will be printed and sent posthaste for your information.*

The *Telefact* provided a voice for national and regional activism. The format contained a memo from the president, NCNW notes, affiliate reports, good news about membership, administrative news and issues needing programmatic attention. From 1943 to 1949, Howard University faculty women Drs. Inabel Lindsay, dean of the School of Social Work; Dorothy B. Ferebee in medicine; Marion Wright Thompson in English; and Flemmie Kittrell, chair of the Department of Home Economics contributed their professional training to NCNW. In 1943, issues addressed topics such as the purchase of the Washington property, property renovations, visitors to the house, wartime efforts for Negro women and job clinics. With a suggestion from Bethune and a motion from attorney Edith Sampson of Chicago—seconded by Sadie T.M. Alexander of Philadelphia—the executive committee, board of directors and legal committee of NCNW passed the motion resulting in the purchase of the building. The December 1943 *Telefact* reported:

> *This was a most historic occasion. Women came from several sections of the country with love, interest, and the determination to raise the status of Negro women in every possibly way. The women gave thanks and praise to the President Bethune who had vision enough to secure a building to house our national headquarters. Mrs. Harriet Curtis Hall, from Boston made the excellent suggestion that organizations, or individuals furnish a room, or rooms, or give a piece of furniture in memory of someone. Dr. Dorothy B. Ferebee made the excellent suggestion that we all buy shares of love and interest in the Council Building. These shares would not declare dividends, but would give the women a chance to share in the buying of our permanent headquarters.* [These] *suggestions were heartily accepted and those who bought shares will be named.*

Howard University's Hilyard Robinson, a notable architect, was contracted to renovate the building. A roster of guests listed Prince Ecket Udong of Nigeria, West Africa, and Dr. Charlotte Hawkins Brown of Sedalia, North Carolina. "The Council is always very happy to receive its friends, and to let them know what we are on the beam." The quest for wartime employment and skills training for Negro women occupied a large section of the 1943 *Telefact*. It published the Negro War Worker's Pledge, which admonished workers to carry themselves with dignity as citizens able to accomplish their duties, vowing, "As a Negro war worker, I know that my job I am performing every day is contributing to the Victory of my country in a war to guarantee four fundamental freedoms to people of every race, color and creed. I know, also, I am contributing to a record which will prove to the world that Negroes are efficient and dependable workers."

The pledges were signed and collected at 1812 Ninth Street, Northwest, in the Department of Employment, the earlier headquarters of NCNW. Bethune and NCNW did not waste any opportunity to defeat segregation and stereotypes through action. They announced a Wartime Employment

Clinic and Hold Your Job week to ensure that Negroes were prepared and informed about employment. The workshops sought to preempt any postwar reduction in Negro employment. NCNW strongly urged its councils and affiliates to continue workshops. "Although Hold Your Job Week is over the National Committee strongly urges everyone to continue [the] program. The Committee feels that this type of program is another front on which the Negro must fight. In addition to getting new and better jobs, and in addition to helping solve the problems of discrimination and segregation, there is the responsibility devolved upon workers to keep the gains made as a result of these efforts by seeing to it that their behavior and work habits are good." The *Telefact* printed comments from Howard University's Dr. Inabel Lindsay, who served as the national chairman of the Postwar Planning Committee of NCNW. "It is particularly significant to members of minority groups in these democracies that they can speak frankly in urging greater recognition and opportunity to share the privileges of a complete democracy. TO CONSERVE WHATEVER GAINS MADE NOW, AND TO USE THESE AS A FOUNDATION FOR A JUST AND PROSPEROUS PEACE, POST-WAR PLANNING BECOMES OF PARAMOUNT IMPORTANCE."

In 1944, *Telefact* published information about a black airline company, efforts to pay the mortgage, Bethune's testimony before FEPC hearings, the SS *Harriet Tubman*, an interracial meeting, Hold Your Job clinics and international guests and interests, as well as vignettes from the building dedication. Union Air Lines, a Washington-based black-owned commercial airline operated by William H. Hawkins, christened its first plane *Mary Bethune* in Griffith Stadium in Washington, D.C. This honor was noted in the *Telefact* so members of the NCNW could know the impact their president had on Negro businesses.

The commentary from the dedication of the property displays the passion and purpose of the NCNW headquarters:

This building is dedicated to the united service of the women of America and the world, regardless of creed, class or color. A place where women can meet and secure current and discerning information, facts and sound direction. Here women of all nationalities can come together without fear or hesitancy secure in the knowledge that they meet as equals and as workers striving together. We can think together, objectively and opportunely and coordinate for the greater benefit of mankind all the able and fine things that women are doing. And finally, to take action swiftly and with deep purpose in the name of our common humanity. We had no time for social gestures yesterday. The times are too intemperate for that. More and more of our women are preparing themselves and other women to understand and possess immovable convictions about the kind of a world that they want for themselves and their children. United and strong, Negro women will do their share in the realization of a new world by the decisions that they make today.

Concurrently, the celebration of the property was plagued with difficulty finding funds within the membership to subsidize the costs. During 1944, the Worry Bird, a cartoon character, made his first appearance. He symbolized the financial pressure the NCNW faced and urged the membership to take ownership in paying for the building.

Now the biggest worry I have on hand is the FINANCIAL worry. Last month in the TELEFACT, we announced that shares of LOVE and INTEREST in our new building were available and urged women to buy them. You told me that women and women's organization would be falling over one another eager to buy them. But, I'm here to tell you "I TOLD YOU SO." Not a one wrote a peep about one single share. Didn't I tell you that women were not alert to the importance of a permanent headquarters for Negro women to the extent that they would support it financially, and didn't I tell you that in spite of the fact that other national women's groups have a home and a good program whereby they can plan and fight for the rights of their group, that our women would sput and spurt and say "She this, and she that" and keep us from going places as a group? But you would have it your way, you said you believed in the women; you said you just KNEW they wouldn't let the President go out and beg money to sustain something that they would benefit from. You said you just KNEW that at least all of the officers would take out Life Memberships or buy shares, because they were our leaders...Let me tell you BUD, you were dead wrong all around, not even a penny postal card. I wish you would stop getting us all enthused over your predictions unless you know something. Do you really think 1944 will bring an awakening to our members? Oh, I hope so. Because if this keeps up, I'll need six more birds to help me worry where the dough is coming from to keep going. We simply cannot afford to let our President keep on begging for us.

The Worry Bird appeared at a time when Bethune faced health challenges. She suffered from chronic asthma, and a severe bout waylaid her in Daytona for several weeks. Thus the Worry Bird's appearance stimulated a response. In a subsequent issue, the Chicago council sent $500, while Detroit remitted $70. Individual members Madame Sara Spencer Washington gave $25, Dr. Charlotte Hawkins Brown pledged $100 and Major Harriet West gave $20 to the building fund. Little by little, the building's indebtedness was melting. Monies for the building came from soldiers of the 380th, 352nd and 482nd Port Battalions serving in Persia. The men pooled their monies and donated $603 to the building. Bethune published her thanks in the *Telefact*.

Oh how I wish I could call everyone of you by name on behalf of the [NCNW], and say thank you, God bless you! We are deeply touched by the monetary expression of faith and confidence you have in our efforts. It presents a direct challenge to the women to pull together much harder for a democratic world. You have lifted a load from my tired shoulders and you have made the burden easier for our women...We shall continue to fight on the home front so that when you return, you will not have fought in vain. May God bless you and protect everyone of you. When I think of the boys on the battle front and the difficulties they are facing, yet thinking in terms of the efforts of our women at home trying to prepare themselves for the complete integration of the womanhood of America and the world; when I think of the years of service our women have given in helping to inspire youth and pointing the way to a life of service, it brings a feeling of a day's work well done.

Political activity for Bethune involved voter education and demanding fairness within legislation. In September 1944, she testified before the FEPC hearings committee:

These women (Negro) feel a particular responsibility for their men serving in the Armed Forces of the United States...These women are concerned that their children live in a post-war world where they may have an opportunity for training for advancement and for work on the basis of their ability and potentialities...The right to work is after all the right to live...Our minorities must not find themselves again handicapped by race, religion, color or national origin...The Congress of the United States must take the lead in abolishing discrimination in employment.

The FEPC was a concession of President Roosevelt, who opted for conciliation with black activists such as A. Philip Randolph and others who suffered economic injustice as a result of being locked out of trade unions and subject to lower pay scales. Bethune added her voice of displeasure to a growing chorus of leaders who knew that the government could stem the tide of economic injustice with legislation.

Concurrently, NCNW remained patriotic to the war effort. NCNW funded and launched the SS *Harriet Tubman*. Through a $2,000,000 war bond rally, the organization paid for a liberty ship. "It will mean that the spirit of Harriet Tubman again has rallied to the cause of freedom, and that you personally played a big part in liberating the ship named for a great woman." In July 1944, an interracial baseball game at Griffith Stadium hosted a war bond rally at which Major Harriet West, Dean William Pickens, a choir of boy scouts and others sold bonds. NCNW raised the funds needed and launched the SS *Harriet Tubman* in summer 1944. The *Aframerican Journal* dedicated an issue to the SS *Harriet Tubman*. The SS *Harriet Tubman* was the only liberty ship that served in World War II named after a black woman. It launched on June 3, 1944. There were 2,711 liberty ships, of which only 18 were named for black Americans. Tubman, born enslaved, acquired her freedom through the Underground Railroad and returned numerous times to liberate nearly three hundred other enslaved people. During the Civil War, she provided valuable service to the Union forces. For Bethune and the NCNW, Tubman's heroism and patriotism befitted the World War II effort; thus they purchased the ship and dubbed it the SS *Harriet Tubman*.

In February 1944, NCNW participated in an interracial conference. The all-day meeting gathered women's organizations, and Eleanor Roosevelt was a guest speaker. Jewish, American, Indian, Mexican and Negro women convened to examine discrimination in the armed forces, housing, health and economics.

Although interracial meetings of organizations are not an unusual event since they have been called together often, this is the first time that national women's organizations have met voluntarily to consider the problem. The following statement was issued from the Conference: "Recognizing the strength in numbers and moral power that lies in the national organizations of women, representatives of thirty national organizations met to discuss 'Building Better Race Relationships.' We recognize that discrimination, lack of opportunity and injustice based on race, color, creed and country of origin constitutes the greatest danger to national unity on the home front and a denial of dignity of the human individual."

Bethune and others realized that women held a unique position in society. Their unity across racial lines would instruct children and change society from the bottom up. Moreover, the children exposed to their example would grow into balanced adults who would ideally pursue peace and equity. The NCNW worked to ensure an egalitarian future while engaging the harsh realities of economic injustice. The Hold Your Job workshop in March 1944 realized that Negro women encountered particular problems, such as lack of appropriate employment locations, training facilities, available training and diversity in available types of jobs. To address the root concerns of job equity, the NCNW sought methods and means to provide child care, transportation and housing and to teach professionalism and workplace etiquette. This formula exposed women to needed resources and groomed them for better positions. The local councils were encouraged to host a magazine dinner, journal tea or public meeting where members of the Negro press could discuss matters of housing, employment and economics. Informed women were better equipped to engage the future as well as lift those women struggling in their communities.

The harsh economic realities of wartime employment did not restrict the *Telefact* from acknowledging social events, such as the visit of Sarah Simpson George of Monrovia, Liberia, the wife of Samuel D. George of the House of Representatives in Liberia. The *Telefact* recognized the need for solidarity with the Women's Work Association (WWA) of Addis Ababa, Ethiopia, through Princess Tanagne-Work, president of WWA. Bethune wrote, "We, the [NCNW], are desirous of knowing you and your women better, and wish for you success in your work. [You and the WWA are welcome to visit the NCNW building when in the United States.]"

In 1945 and 1946, the issues addressed contained greater levity. There was discussion about changing the name of the Council. The rise of liberal thought and integration made some question the relevance of remaining named the National Council of Negro Women. Bethune and others did not view "Negro" as a dated or narrow term. Clearly, the issue was tabled, and the NCNW remained aptly named. Often visitors to the House were women passing through to other places, including: Dr. Beulah Winston, Dean of Women at Clark University in Atlanta, Georgia, who was heading to the Girl Scouts of America meeting; and Dorothy Lymas and T.C. Washington, who were off to attend a peace conference. Edmonia W.

Grant, public relations adviser to the American Missionary Association and Pusheng Kung, Chinese representative of EAST-WEST Association also visited. Hubert Dillworth, a baritone from New York who was in a local Washington show called *Bloomer Girl*, visited the House for tea and provided an impromptu concert of several musical selections. Mrs. Netta Paulyn Garner, an NCNW member and pianist from Los Angeles, also performed an informal concert for a small audience.

The Worry Bird did not appear in 1945 or 1946. Seemingly, the fundraising efforts of Daisy Lampkin resulted in $50,000 of the $55,000 drive. Other contributors mentioned included Ethel Watkins Sissel, who collected $1,900, while Jane Spaulding raised $1,000 in West Virginia—a state without a NCNW council. Bethune wrote:

> *On behalf of the members of NCNW, I wish to express the appreciation of the efforts of these fine women and all other participants and contributors. Their efforts will enable the NCNW to embark upon a real and effective program for womanhood. WE ARE DEBT FREE!! THANK YOU!! Aren't you glad? The most outstanding achievement of the year is ownership of our Council Headquarters. It is free from debt in less than two years. We bring our warmest gratitude to our member organizations, Metropolitan Councils, Officers, Life Members and friends, who have cooperated with us in this accomplishment. Let us thank God for the strength and wisdom that has been given us to bring this to pass.*

The pride in Negro history inspired Delta Sigma Theta, Bethune's sorority, to sponsor a tea to present female Negro authors. Books written by and about Negroes were displayed, and copies were donated to the Council library. "This marks only the beginning of our project to assemble materials significant in the life of Negro womanhood. We urge each council to solicit books suitable for the library, especially those written by or about women." The formation of an archives and library confirmed the lasting legacy of Bethune, who viewed her work in the tradition of Negro women such as Sojourner Truth, Harriet Tubman and others. The collection of books and artifacts extended the ownership of the House into the past and future of Negro women. This vision was endorsed by Mrs. S.E. Bailey of Arkansas, mother of Sue Bailey Thurman, who provided a donation of $1,000 for the museum.

Nevertheless, NCNW remained vigilant locally and nationally, and it reported, "Racial bigotry remains the rule in the nation's capital, despite the numerous protests from progressive groups. Particularly is this attitude noted in the local theaters where Negroes are consistently denied admission to play houses, even when accompanied by white friends. Our National Convention sent a telegram to Robert Sherwood commending his forthright stand against such discrimination in D.C. theaters. He pledged 33 leading playwrights to refuse to let their plays come to D.C. as long as any part of the audience is jim-crowed." The election of the Eightieth Congress stirred concern. "We understand the significance of the election results in terms of future progress and welfare of our citizenry. We urge your vigilance toward issues to be considered by our legislators. Their decisions affect our lives, both directly and indirectly. As intelligent women, we must examine the issues carefully and organize support for every piece of legislation that means a better life for the majority of the people."

Bethune, as a Washington resident, was sensitive to this fact and kept her voting status in New York. Washington residents and their voting rights were often the subjects of political debates. Leadership in the city and the proximity to the federal government precluded the city from becoming a state. The *Telefact* noted that Senator Theodore M. Bilbo was the "self-styled mayor of Washington," and his agenda was vocally against democracy for Negroes at the cost of the larger city. The political climate changed with the death of President Roosevelt. His death in 1945 impacted Bethune and NCNW, as they lost a confidant and an ally. President Truman ushered in a new era of politics that allowed NCNW to engage the civil rights agenda from a female perspective. Roosevelt's FEPC faced a filibuster in the Senate. An open letter implored members to consider the possibility of life with the FEPC. Membership needed to accelerate efforts to press President Truman's Wage Hour Act and Full Employment Bill to retain economic gains since the war. The national outcome provided reprieve for military personnel, but private industry would take decades to conform.

In 1947, there were four full presidential messages. The September and October messages explained plans for the NCNW convention. In February's message, Bethune explained her dual role as administrator of Bethune-Cookman College and NCNW president. The postwar period found her involved in the educational careers of 670 students, of whom 375 were veterans. While in Washington, growing responsibility outpaced the financial contributions. Bethune wrote in the *Telefact*:

> *We shall continue undaunted to press for those programs and principles which may be secured through the democratic processes…improving the lot*

of minorities all over the world…lean heavily upon each one of you to hold up our arms in this critical period. Even though we are scattered from the Atlantic to the Pacific, we can gather strength by joining hands in one great bond of fellowship that binds us together in our common program. Great courage, faith, creative ability and zeal, to continue our united efforts to work for better understanding among all groups, are needed. You can depend upon me in the future as in the past to give leadership and guidance which you direct according to my strength and ability.

Aging and battling chronic asthma and other health issues, Bethune relinquished control of her school, yet her presence and house on campus remained. Her Daytona property was a fixture on campus and served as her last residence. Hints of this reality are evident in her May-June president's message.

I have just ended the most challenging, the [hardest] worked, yet a most triumphant year at my desk in Florida. God and man have been most kind to me. I am glad that a President has been found for the College. I returned to my desk in Washington. I do hope most sincerely that the great heat waves…have not effected too deeply the spirit and the programs of the women of the Council…The problems of local and national security, and of world leadership and cooperation are stirring the country as never before. We must understand the issues involved, in order to lend our support to the right interpretation of the programs and policies…We must have within our reach, at a time like this, strength, courage, wisdom and means with which to carry on, in order that we may together make a worthwhile contribution to the great task that has been assigned to the womanhood of the world. Some of us are tired and weary, but those are not the moments to shirk or to give up. We must continue to fight until the battle is won.

In the wake of World War II, many black military personnel returned with hope of good employment and greater freedom as American citizens. Unfortunately, the ugliness of segregation and discrimination impeded full expressions of black citizenship. Throughout the south, moments of violence occurred when social norms met with black resistance bubbling up with long-held desires for freedom. The late 1940s produced ripe moments that burst open in the 1950s. Black Americans would not allow another generation to swallow their dreams because of race. Bethune, a daughter of the nineteenth century, viewed her contribution to the proto–Civil Rights movement as that of a time-tested activist. Through the NCNW's publications, she added her voice to the chorus of dissent and displeasure while energizing young women to action. Alongside political statements, *Telefact* listed visitors to the House. Of note is Ora Brown Stokes, NCNW parliamentarian. Stokes attended the Women's Christian Temperance Union (WCTU) meeting, where she was made an honorary life member in part because of her activities as a field secretary and consultant on interracial affairs on behalf of the WCTU.

In 1948, a number of events occurred at the House. A diplomatic reception honoring Ambassador Charles of Haiti and Mrs. King of Liberia was attended by five hundred guests who filtered through the event. It was sponsored by a cross-section of women's groups from Baltimore and Washington demonstrating the success of cooperative events. A concurrent event was held June 13: a reception for the "Women of the Year" and the dedication of the Bailey Memorial Room in honor of the late S.E. Bailey, whose donation aided in augmenting the archives. Despite these successes, a financial report showed a shortfall of income. At the same time, Olivia Henry Supreme Basileus of Phi Delta Kappa presented NCNW with a check for $700 for back dues and a pledge. Financial matters plagued NCNW, and another message from the editor sought to rouse the membership to greater fiscal commitment:

> *I wish that each of you could have the opportunity of working day by day with our President Mrs. Bethune. To say that "she is wonderful" is an understatement. She is the most extraordinary and divinely guided person I have ever met. I am saying this now and here, women, for I believe in as I have never believed before, and I see as I have never seen before—HER VISION OF FIRST CLASS CITIZENSHIP, AND DIGNITY OF WOMANHOOD, FOR US, the brown American women of this country. She has given us the strongest vehicle for making this vision clear. My only hope is that before it is too late, we will "wake-up," and really make our Council strong in finances and program. We can no longer depend upon Mrs. Bethune to "carry us around." We are intelligent women, we are mature women, we are trained women, we are experienced women. As such let us, under her guidance, make our Council a LIVE AND STRONG force for justice and freedom for all women. God has been wonderful to us to give us a leader like Mrs. Bethune. Let us give "THANKS" by listening to, and working with her for our common good.*

In April, Bethune's president's message inaugurated the Memorial to Forward March of Women.

> *All my life I have wanted to see here in Washington, a building for all women in which offices, reception rooms and concert hall facilities will be adequate, beautiful and dignified. Our Memorial will be open to all women of all races, and will afford facilities ranking with those of any organization in Washington. In it, the women of our land may feel free to meet, to bring their guests without apologies, explanations and hesitancy. In it, only the spirit of prejudice and intolerance will be barred. During my life, God has granted me much achievement and opportunity. It has been my struggle to use these gifts unselfishly and with great perspective. In these final years of my life, I dare to work for the dream of a memorial for all women because the time has come for it, and it is a cause worth every sacrifice.*

Bethune concluded that the current location was too small. She viewed property in Dupont Circle and desired a larger space for NCNW. However, the property sale was impeded by a group of select white women. In April 1948, NCNW faced "unexplained opposition on the part of high-placed Episcopalians" in acquiring the former home of Mabel Boardman at Eighteenth and P Streets, northwest. Boardman was involved with the Red Cross and sought to sell her home. "According to unconfirmed reports the Episcopal Foundation with whom the deal was being made yielded to pressure from elements in the Episcopal group that opposed admitting the Negro organization into the neighborhood." Eleanor Roosevelt supported Bethune's endeavor while Episcopal Bishop Angus Dunn was cool on the evolving deal. Bethune stated, "It is my hope to establish in Washington a beautiful, elaborate and fitting memorial in keeping with the forward march of our women. In setting up this permanent monument I feel we should get beyond the fringes [and] aim for the heights of elegance and refinement." Ultimately, NCNW's offer of a $150,000 down payment was rejected, and the Boardman house temporarily taken off the market.

Unable to occupy a larger space, people still frequented the House. Guests included Senator Claude Pepper; Congressman William L. Dawson; Mr. S. Cala of Havana, Cuba; and Rackham Holt, along with 1,500 other guests in the spring of 1948. *Telefact* published a statement to encourage potential visitors: "the Council makes its facilities available to all women's organizations for conferences, forums, club meetings, receptions and all wholesome entertainments." Other events at the House were sponsored by the intercultural committee, which hosted a meet-the-author gathering where Abel Pleen spoke on his book *Southern Americas*. "This event was the first of a series of events designed by the Committee to strengthen the good neighbor policy between the Americas. More than 100 persons greeted Pleen." The intercultural committee sponsored a Fellowship Party for students of all countries at the House. "It was a beautiful sight to see students from other countries dressed in their native costumes mingling, playing, chatting and exchanging experiences with students from University of Maryland, Howard, Catholic and American Universities, Minor Teachers College and others. A perfect example of democratic living."

Carol Brice, a noted coloratura soprano, offered to perform a benefit concert for the NCNW in Washington at Constitution Hall owned by the Daughters of the American Revolution (DAR). The DAR refused to rent the space to the NCNW because of a clause in the contract that stipulated the audience be solely white. Brice, Bethune and the NCNW decided to move the concert to New York's Carnegie Hall. Bethune used the opportunity to promote the concert as a fund- and consciousness-raising event. She promoted the concert as one for civil and human rights in direct protest of the DAR and in full support of the NCNW's agenda. The concert did not produce the expected revenue; however, it did shame the DAR, which ultimately changed its policy in the 1950s.

In 1949, the *Telefact* announced associate membership for men. The associate members had no voice in the administrative affairs of the Council but would be able to assist in underwriting and perpetuating its activities and might serve as consultants.

Bethune sought to identify someone to assume the presidency of the Council, and Dr. Ferebee was her obvious choice. Her capacity in directing AKA and providing considerable support to Bethune during her presidency resulted in her being elected to the presidency of the NCNW. Ferebee's presidency integrated a number of projects focusing on health and wellness. She also served as Council treasurer and understood the need for funding and fundraising. The NCNW sought to provide adequate health facilities and service for all. Through the support of President Truman's National Health Program, the NCNW lent its expertise and infrastructure to ensure that organizations supporting Negro women and girls received the funding necessary for appropriate healthcare.

Telefact mentioned a number of international activities. Latin America, Haiti, Germany and India were mentioned. The annual Cuban reception for goodwill was successful. The reception was highlighted by a series of short speeches aimed to tell the Cuban visitors about the life of the Negro in America. Speakers were Dr. Dorothy Ferebee for the National Council, Mrs. Thomasina Herford, Mr. Emmer Lancaster, Madame Lillian Evanti and Henry S. Grillo. Concurrently, the conditions in Ecuador concerned NCNW. The Ecuador Relief Fund sought to raise funds for earthquake victims. The NCNW, along with the Organization of American States (OAS), appealed to American citizens to aid disaster survivors. There were 100,000 people left homeless after the earthquake, and many were suffering transportation difficulties and in need of basic supplies. The OAS welcomed monetary donations to purchase supplies, and the NCNW sought to contribute to its cause. A subsequent note urged membership to learn a new pledge: "IT IS OUR PLEDGE to make a lasting contribution to all that is finest and best in America, so that her heritage of freedom and progress will be infinitely enriched by the integration of all of her people (regardless of racial, creedal or national origin) into the economic, social, cultural, civic and political life of their country and thus achieve the glorious destiny of a true and unfettered democracy."

In August, at age seventy-four, Bethune visited Haiti. Haiti's successful war for independence liberated the island nation in 1791 from the French colonizers. The successful slave revolts placed the country outside of economic development as punishment for ousting the French colonial rulers. Bethune's visit linked the black American and Haitian liberation struggles for economic self-sufficiency. During her visit, she attended the Haitian Congress in Port-Au-Prince. Bethune suggested the NCNW aid the country financially. The industrious Haitian people utilized their skills to provide for their people. Agriculture, home industries and scientific forestry inched the country out of poverty. Bethune was eager to see the benefits from small business opportunities as well as outside funds offered to public and private enterprise. Bethune stated, "Let us continue to press and work until the doors of full opportunity re-open to the Haitian people...I would like to give seventy-four years more in helping them to demonstrate to the world what can be done for democracy in that paradise—that land of beauty."

NCNW reported the travel of Edith Sampson to Germany. Sampson was a member of the NCNW Executive Committee and traveled on its behalf. Chester Williams, director of the World Town Hall Seminar, provided a letter to the Council describing Sampson's contributions to the town hall. "Everyone loves her and is delighted to have such a fine-spirited woman as a companion on this tour. She is doing a vast amount of good for Negro women and for the country we all love…In Berlin she was such a good sport that she struggled through a broadcast in German. At various times along the way she has risen to the occasion with just the right note and important expressions of the views of Negro Women." Sampson participated in the Round the World town meeting in London, England, which was broadcast as *American Abroad* on NBC. Mrs. Vijaya Pandit, a NCNW life member, served as the Indian Ambassador to Russia and America. Locally, a Washington Theater Festival provided unsegregated open-air seating. "To witness the opening of the eight weeks of drama under the stars were many Washingtonians of all races, creeds and classes…Among the host of distinguished patrons attending were Representatives Edith N. Rogers, R., Mass; Mrs. Estes Kefauver, Senator Irving Ives, R., N.Y; Mrs. Bethune, Dr and Mrs. Mordecai Johnson, Mr. and Mrs. Melvin Hildreth and Ambassadors from Italy, Canada, Norway, Mexico, Peru, Chile and Austria."

Finally, the intercultural committee reported events where international students and government leaders exchanged information. In February, Mrs. Clavender Bright of Liberia talked about the lives and problems of Liberian women. The second-annual fellowship for foreign students represented countries from the Caribbean, Africa and Europe, demonstrating that people can work and play together regardless of their national origin. The December 1949 issue of *Telefact* marked the end of Bethune's administration. Bethune stepped aside in light of challenges from aging. Over her forty years of influence, she had created a school and national organization. Moving from active duty to a supervisory role allowed her to remain connected and involved without the physical and emotional stress inherent in the position of president.

Out of my heart at Christmas time comes a deeper and more sincere appreciation for friends and coworkers who have made life worth living. Looking back over the 14 years of service we have given together in the National Council, I thank God for your friendship, your cooperation and your support. I ask that you will give to our new President and her cabinet all of the assistance, cooperation and prayers needed in the execution of our expanded program. I know I can count upon you to help keep the Council a dignified and effective force for good in the service of mankind.

In 1949, a biographical sketch of Dr. Dorothy Ferebee ran that detailed her credentials:

> *A woman of broad interests and high capabilities…a practicing physician in D.C. Acting Director of the University Health Service, Howard University…Born in Virginia, reared and educated in Massachusetts. Grand-niece of Josephine St. Pierre Ruffin, who was fearless President of the Woman's Era Club of Boston in 1895…Former national president of Alpha Kappa Alpha Sorority, and for 6 years was Medical Director for its Mississippi Health Project. Founded the Southeast Settlement House in D.C., and was president for 13 years…By her training and background, Dr. Ferebee brings a wealth of experience and information to the National Council.*

Aware of Bethune's vision and the benefits of collective action, she continued to move the NCNW forward. Her holiday address extended warm greetings of friendship and kinship. Building a national organization and empowering various branches required constant information and strategy. Through the *Telefact* newsletter, members communicated and coordinated their efforts. Moreover, they were allowed to celebrate their accomplishments.

PRESERVING NEGRO WOMEN'S HISTORY

The publications documented the contemporary life of the NCNW and Negro women, while the archives and library preserved the larger memory of the Negro experience. Bethune was interested in sharing the documentary evidence of progress Negro women had made. Her childhood and the stories of her mother and grandmother impressed her deeply, impelling her to offer similar stories to younger women. Joyce Hanson wrote, "[Bethune] credited Patsy's and Sophie's example for giving her determination to work racial equality…[They] were instrumental in shaping [her] perspective on [the role of women] in racial advancement."

> *Much collecting, interpreting, and disseminating data of interest to black women…By 1949, constitutionally, the council was also to "preserve information particularly affecting women. On June 30, 1946, it advanced this goal through the observance of National Archives Day,*

complete with a brochure detailing ways it could be celebrated. Vice President Estelle Massy Riddle Osborne publicized that it was "a project designed to give impetus to the building of a National Museum at the Council House—where the records, letters, books, pictures, medals and other authentic materials, suggestive of the struggles and accomplishments of Negro women can be assembled."

Dorothy Porter, Howard librarian, and Dr. Carter G. Woodson, a historian, were collecting documentary evidence of Negro life and culture across the diaspora. However, neither Porter nor Woodson solely focused on women in light of the larger neglect Negro history experienced. In the 1940s, Negro history was principally documented and written from the outside—a perspective that positioned them as victims rescued by white heroes. Therefore, accurate telling of the history required librarians and historians to collect authentic accounts of Negro life from the material evidence they had created and left behind. The archives committee included archivists, anthropologists and historians. The scholars provided the criteria for the archives. The committee created included: Mary Church Terrell, Dr. Woodson, Dr. Charlotte Brown, Mr. Harcourt Tynes, Mrs. Dorothy Porter, Miss Jane Hunter, Mr. Earl Conrad, Dr. Charles Johnson, Dr. E. Franklin Frazier and Dr. Margaret Meade. Bethune, with leadership from Thurman, formally launched a collecting campaign. Delta Sigma Theta joined the call and sponsored author talks and teas, as well as book drives to collect works by and about Negro women. The limited space at the house forced the library to serve as a conference room and boardroom when necessary.

For many black organizations, maintaining archives and special collections was desired, but appropriate space was a common obstacle. Woodson maintained the Associated Publishers and the Association for the Study of Negro Life and History (ASNLH) business and research materials in his house until he purchased a facility to provide greater space. Thurman was committed to the vision of a library and archives. She requested each local council donate a black doll "who would be named for a regional or national black woman" and accompanied by a biographical statement. "The [NCNW's] Library and Museum Committee had already received a nice cache of items. It possessed one hundred commemorative stamps of the seventy-fifth anniversary of the Thirteenth Amendment...It had newspaper clippings, historic clothes, an identity locket from the slavery era, a veteran's Civil War medal...[and] Bethune's Spingarn Medal."

Mrs. Bethune dedicates the Bailey Memorial Room at the NCNW house. *Courtesy Mary McLeod Bethune Council House, NPS.*

The dedication of Thurman to the archives initiative cultivated a "preservation sensitive" culture within the NCNW. The NCNW affiliate organizations and membership were encouraged to celebrate living heroines as well as document achievements through publishing in the *Telefact* or *Aframerican Journal* or welcomed to submit items for deposit in the archives. In May 1946, Vivian Carter Mason instructed Bethune in a letter to secure permissions for a Wings Over Jordan radio program on which Thurman was scheduled to speak about NCNW's archives. Mason also suggested that Bethune provide copies of program transcripts to be sent to ministers, school principals, organizational heads, librarians and newspapers.

The National Archives Day inaugurated the formal collecting of significant, unusual and rare documentary evidence of the accomplishments of Negro women in the development of the social, economic, political and cultural patterns of life. The desired end result was to spread knowledge about the contributions of Negro women whose pride, courage and impetus contributed to the development of Negro people. The national day would have a two-prong approach, a national and local structure. The national program involved:

*Nation-wide hook-up on "The Negro Woman Marches On"—
"In the Vanguard," "Negro Women, Heroines All" as a theme on
[popular] radio programs...Ask national organizations such as the
National Board of the YWCA, National Council of Jewish Women,
National Council of Catholic Women, Federation of Women's Clubs,
NAACP, National Urban League, the CIO of AFL, Federal Council
of Churches, United Council of Church Women to observe in any
way that they can National Archives Day. Especially, to publicize in
their official organs a statement concerning the contributions of Negro
women of yesterday and today (We can furnish suggested materials).
Give releases to all newspapers. Ask women columnists to try [and]
write an article or use some part of the material in their column that
day or during the week.*

The local program involved organizing listening parties around the
national broadcast. Each council received a brochure, which they were
encouraged to share with their ministers, local papers and schools. It was
suggested that they host events in public school libraries or honor a local
woman of past or present accomplishment to reinforce the importance of
the archives. The event sought to promote the archives and NCNW as well
as raise money for collecting materials.

On June 17, 1946, in an interview on WINX radio, Bethune spoke about
the formation of Archives Day and explained its purpose:

*National Archives Day—a project designed to give impetus to the building
of a National Museum at [the] Council House—where the records,
letters, books, pictures, medals and other authentic materials, suggestive of
the struggles and accomplishments of Negro women, can be assembled.
We want, through such a collection, to tell in concrete form the story of the
contributions of Negro women to American life...As early as 1773, Negro
women were active in our national life. Phyllis Wheatley, the first American
Negro women poet, told in her volume of poems on various subjects of her
contact with General George Washington.*

Bethune continued to mention the exploits of Negro women such as
Harriet Tubman and Sojourner Truth. The interviewer queried about
Negro women being the last hired and first fired. Bethune responded:

All hands are pressed into service to get out the post-convention mailing. *Courtesy Mary McLeod Bethune Council House, NPS.*

Unfortunately, this is too often true. The Negro woman more than any other woman in America has had to face discrimination in the matter of jobs. Handicapped as are all women because of sex, the Negro woman has the added obstacle of discrimination against her because of race—the latter has been the more difficult to overcome. She is still a marginal worker. However, during [World War II], many new fields of employment were opened to her with the added opportunity to gain new skills and develop new abilities. It was during this period that her abilities were recognized, and we now fight to help her keep the gains she has made.

Bethune acknowledged that the economic boon of wartime industry could erode, thus NCNW fought to secure permanent employment and lifelong job training skills. The concerns about Negro women and employment were directly related to the archives initiative. Bethune understood the connection between the past and present as experienced through her childhood. Archives

Day served as a nationwide program publicizing the contributions of Negro women for younger women and larger society.

Bethune concluded in the radio interview, "Locally, an 'Author's Tea' is being planned at the [House] by Delta Sigma Theta Sorority, an affiliate of our organization. At this time, Negro women authors and their works will be presented. Similar celebrations will take place throughout the country. We are urging all groups to share this project so that a record of these achievements will become a permanent treasure—an inspiration to future generations."

Concurrently, Thurman presented a program on WWDC radio station on June 29, 1946, on the initiation of the National Negro Women's Archives and Museum Department. The program provided historical vignettes about notable Negro women. Thurman allowed the listener to understand the purpose of NCNW through a brief historical sketch. The 1935 NCNW pledge provides a logical foundation for the archives: "It is our pledge to make a lasting contribution to all that is finest and best in America, so that her heritage of freedom and progress will be infinitely enriched by the integration of 14 million Negroes into the economic, social, cultural, civic and political life of their country and thus achieve the glorious destiny of a true and unfettered Democracy." Thurman, like Bethune, knew that history informed the present. The rising generations of young Negro women needed to know the fortitude of their foremothers as well as the obstacles encountered in the quest for social justice. Thurman provided historical sketches of Phyllis Wheatley, Sojourner Truth and Harriet Tubman. She also mentioned lesser-known women such as Mary Jane Paterson, the first Negro woman to receive a college degree; Sarah M. Loguen, a graduate in medicine; and Elizabeth Keckley, the fashion designer who dressed Mary Lincoln. Thurman ended with a list of contemporary Negro female "firsts": Judge Jane Bolin, the first in New York state; Pauli Murray, deputy assistant to the attorney general in California; and Crystal Bird Fauset, state legislator in Pennsylvania. Thurman stated:

We have in our attic trunks, no doubt, newspaper stories and accounts of important achievements and accomplishments of Negro women in all communities, wherever we may live, in all parts of the United States. We are asking our friends throughout the country to send us whatever they may discover that will be of value to the National Archives of Negro Women... The Council House will be extended to include a [archives] which will become an important shrine in the Nation's Capital. The impetus for promoting this shrine has come through the recent gift to the Council from Negro woman whose life has been devoted to the ideal that the future of any race or nation must be established on the records of the past, and that only as we know and appreciate our history, can we put ground under our feet.

Thurman's passion for archives stemmed in part from her mother's donation to NCNW. Her donation of $1,000 came despite her humble beginnings. Thurman's mother worked as a schoolteacher in the 1880s. In the summer/fall 1940 edition of *Aframerican*, Thurman's mother was noted as one who "used her modest income through the years to help dozens of brilliant young men and women receive education in the best schools of the country and [aided] in the development of college and community libraries in [Arkansas]." The perpetual gift of education manifested in the NCNW archives.

In an article titled "The Greatest of These," Thurman recounted the activities of the seventh NCNW conference. Thurman wrote:

[It] *was easy to tell the story in terms of creative achievement: for the very first time, perhaps, five generations of Negro women conferred together in an atmosphere of personal camaraderie. Teen-age Girl Scouts were on the floor as ushers when Hallie Q. Brown, the veteran educator who was a close comrade of Frederick Douglass, made her stirring address. Lawyers were there, fully twelve in number, forming a most capable and articulate group. One of these, whose mother was in the organization of the National Association of Colored Women, now holds the position of assistant District Attorney for the State of New York, and recently received the honorary Doctor of Laws degree from Smith College, her Alma Mater...The group of women physicians was led by the brilliant one who established through a certain prominent sorority, the famous health clinics in Mississippi. She was associated of course, with the Director of Nurses of Homer Phillips Hospital in St. Louis...a person of amazing capacities who travels unceasingly in interest of improving the health of a very important sector of our Nation. There were educators—women who had founded schools and mothered the women's movement in part engendered by those schools. This group included three distinguished persons; the Founder and President of the Council, the First Vice President of the 1941 conference, and the Corresponding Secretary of the National Baptist Women of America...There were social workers, women of the Press, business executives, public school teachers...The*

Women, including Mrs. Bethune, Jeanetta Welch Brown, Sue Bailey Thurman and Arabella Denniston, view the newest additions to National Archives for Negro Women's History. *Courtesy Mary McLeod Bethune Council House, NPS.*

> *little eight-year-old will be in years to come the professional descendant of one of the women represented there. But more important to the fortunate ones of her age, is an inheritance from the Body of the Whole, which may come in time to represent the ultimate triumph of that conference... Insight, Courage, Patience, Vision a composite gift of spirit.*

The success of the NCNW, Thurman believed, resided in the heights attained by young women. The foundations established were moot unless a young person was inspired and impelled to continue racial uplift and community service. Thus, the House provided a living memorial to accomplishment yet to be recorded—however, expected by contemporary occupants stewarding the dreams of Negro women.

CHAPTER 3

In the House

Bethune's use of the House sought to involve the entire Negro community and larger world of womanhood. To commemorate the success of the property and growth of NCNW, Bethune crafted an award to acknowledge outstanding women. In 1944, she held a press conference and announced the NCNW's honor roll award. The honor roll celebrated accomplishments of women whose selflessness promoted peace, progress and human rights. In announcing the inaugural 1944 nominees, she expressed concern for the lack of recognition women both white and Negro received from organizations and the media: "[W]ith [our] men at war, more women than ever have taken up responsibilities in every field of endeavor and have made significant contributions to American life." For the next five years, NCNW reviewed nominations and selected seventy-one white, Negro, domestic and foreign-born women, highlighting their contributions to humanity. The honorees were given certificates and coverage in the *Aframerican Women's Journal* as well as numerous black newspapers in conjunction with a reception held at the House attended by notables, media and the NCNW membership.

CELEBRATING ALL WOMANKIND: THE HONOR ROLL

The 1944 awardees were Eleanor Roosevelt, Anna Arnold Hedgeman, Mary S. Ingram, Mabel Staupers, Alice T. McLean, Daisy Lampkin, Katherine

Shryver, Dorothy Thompson, Lovonia H. Brown, Lillian Smith, Bettye Murphy Phillips, Lena Horne, Dorothy Bellanca, Thomasina M. Johnson, Jeanetta Welch Brown and Pauline Redmond Coggs. In the inaugural group, many of the honorees were involved in aspects of interest to Bethune. Her concerns about women in the military support service, the media, civil rights and innovation often mirrored the activism of those selected. Utilizing the Washington home and NCNW provided confirmation for female pioneers and acknowledged the worthiness of their work. The *Chicago Defender* wrote, "Expressing a concern for the lack of recognition for the achievement of both white and Negro women, as reflected in the various national polls Bethune felt that the role the NCNW plays in the affairs of women qualifies it to place an evaluation on their qualifications." For example, Ms. Smith was the editor of the *South Today*, a publication that fearlessly presented the negative effects of discrimination on human behavior. She also published a book, *Strange Fruit*. Ms. Phillips worked for the *Afro-American* newspaper where she was acknowledged for her informative coverage of the war effort. Entertainer Lena Horne was celebrated for her refusal to appear in stereotypical roles on stage or screen. Executive secretary of the Urban League Coggs fought for Negro housing and racial tolerance in Washington. NCNW's own Brown was fêted for coordinating meetings with diverse groups to eliminate racial animosity and segregation. She was also instrumental in developing the program that resulted in the launching of the SS *Harriet Tubman*. Dorothy Bellanca served as the international vice-president of the Amalgamated Clothing Workers of America. She was celebrated for her effective assistance in the mobilization of female industrial workers. Thomasina M. Johnson served as the legislative representative for the National Non-Partisan Council on Public Affairs, and her success resulted in integration of black women in the WAVEs.

Eleanor Roosevelt was a humanitarian whose "varied activities in the field of human relations, courage, energy and deep concern for national and international unity have given inspiration to women all over the world." The long-term relationship between Bethune and Roosevelt facilitated her selection as a recipient of the award in its first year. Initially she sought moderation for changes in government; however, when she learned of the abuses suffered by black people, she pushed for change. She used her position as first lady to advance the cause of civil rights. She frequented HBCU campuses and flew with the famed Tuskegee Airmen during their training in Alabama. Moreover, she witnessed the American spirit defeat the Depression and Hitlerism, leading her to believe that racism could

On February 10 the National Council of Negro Women honored the sixteen women named on its 1944 Honor Roll at a reception at the Council headquarters in Washington. Shown above and to the left are the honorees. In the top picture are L. to R. Helen Gahagan Douglas, congresswoman from California; Mary McLeod Bethune, president of the National Council of Negro Women; Eleanor Roosevelt, who was chosen the Council's "Woman of the Year"; Lillian Smith, author of "Strange Fruit"; Mabel K. Staupers, Executive Secretary, National Association of Colored Graduate Nurses; Dorothy Bellanco, First Vice-President of the Amalgamated Clothing Workers of America; Daisy Lampkin, Field Representative of the N.A.A.C.P.; Lavonia Brown, President of the Woman's Army for National Defense. Shown in the

Aframerican Women's Journal article with the 1945 Roll of Honor awardees. *Courtesy Mary McLeod Bethune Council House, NPS.*

similarly be destroyed. "She believed wholeheartedly that a democracy must be inclusive and protect minority rights and ensure safe, peaceful protest or cease to be democratic." In line with Bethune, she believed that economic opportunities were essential to racial justice. The hypocrisy of American democracy for her was confirmed in the work of Gunnar Myrdal's *An American Dilemma*. Dr. Myrdal, a Swedish sociologist, examined American culture and concluded that discrimination negatively affected white and black citizens. In *An American Dilemma*, he concluded that the root cause was a conflict in moral values that were contradictory to the American creed of democracy. The solution to the problems of American discrimination lie in white society's free will to embrace all citizens equally. Bethune honored Roosevelt for her selfless commitment to exposing the root of injustice while seeking economic parity for all Americans.

Another inaugural honoree was Mrs. Hedgeman, the executive secretary of the National Committee for the Fair Employment Practices Committee (FEPC). The FEPC originated as Executive Order 8802, which sought to investigate complaints of discrimination within the defense industry receiving federal contracts. President Roosevelt did not fully share his wife's interest in the immediacy of civil rights and only enacted the FEPC after longtime labor leader A. Philip Randolph threatened a 1941 march on Washington of over 100,000 black people to protest discriminatory employment. Hedgeman was selected because of her dynamic leadership in the struggle to secure fair employment through this organization. The all-hands-on-deck mentality during World War II provided employment for many black people, but NCNW was concerned that these gains would evaporate in peacetime. Thus, Hedgeman's role within the FEPC ensured vigilance to black employment. The FEPC was strengthened in 1943 and abolished after the war, never becoming a permanent government agency.

Another recipient, Ms. Mary Ingram, was the president of the national YMCA, and her administration was courageous in developing and implementing interracial practices within the organization. The YMCA and YWCA made up the largest nondenominational organization that provided social services with Christian principles, but the specter of racism crept in, resulting in segregated facilities. Founded in 1866, the Y movement provided Christian men and women with opportunities to volunteer, thus fulfilling their Christian duty to care for the less fortunate. For black Christian women, the desire to provide housing, education and training for young people was essential to ensuring that they would not fall into crime or abusive situations. Many of the services offered by the Y fused practical living with Christian tenets, thus infusing those being served with the understanding that they must serve others. As early as 1873, white women queried whether to offer assistance to "colored" women. The rift between the two groups remained, and both groups served their constituencies through the Y—however, in segregated facilities. Segregation was a bittersweet reality that allowed black Y's to embrace history and culture without a stigma, yet they remained subject to white scrutiny and approval to qualify as an official Y from a principally white national board. In Washington, the Phyllis Wheatley YWCA provided a variety of services and afforded NCNW a space to meet and host events.

Ms. Mabel Staupers was the executive secretary of the National Association of Colored Graduate Nurses (NACGN). The NACGN formed when the white women's group barred Negro women from joining. Bethune recognized Staupers's faithful efforts to secure full utilization of Negro nurses in the war effort. Ms. Daisy Lampkin served as the field secretary for the NAACP. Under her administration, Lampkin grew the membership to the largest in NAACP history. The popularity of the NAACP contributed to its successful and effective fight for equality for all people. Ms. Alice McLean was the founder-president of American Women's Voluntary Services (AWVS). Through the AWVS, McLean contributed to the morale of military service personnel through visits to war theaters. Ms. Katherine Shryver was the executive secretary of the national committee to abolish the poll tax. The poll tax was an extra legal measure used in the segregated south to prevent black people from voting. Shryver employed statesmanlike leadership in legislative and educational campaigns to abolish the corrupt measure. Ms. Dorothy Thompson was a columnist whose political coverage of the 1944 campaigns provided salient analysis of major issues.

Ms. Lovonia Brown, founder and lieutenant general of the Women's Army for National Defense (WANDs), provided leadership in developing programs for military women. Brown created the WANDs after realizing that, though there was a desire by women to participate in the war effort, there was no formal organization for which to volunteer. On November 15, 1942, with nine other women, Brown created the organization, which wrote to Bethune asking for her participation, and she agreed. In a January 1943 letter, Brown expressed her gratitude to Bethune for accepting a role within the WANDs:

> *May I thank you from the depths of my heart for your lovely telegram and letter. It has meant so much to encourage me to go into this movement to*

organize. The women are proud to have your cooperation we feel we are surely to succeed with your very valuable advise [sic] *and guidance…We do want you to be our leader, that is the place we selected for you. The head of any army is called the <u>General</u>, by this endearing title you will be known hereafter by the members of the WANDs. We sent out cards for a meeting last Wed. with your name as our leader, and had* [an] *overwhelming response. It was zero weather but the house was crowded…Your order for uniforms is in the tailors our insignias haven't been finished as yet…Our shoes are black, common sense heel lace tie….No doubt, General Bethune, you will receive many inquiries about your organization after our first publication. Many will seek membership directly from you. We will send blanks and information, but we don't want you to be disturbed too much, you may refer some to this office and we will send out your letters if you desire…You are my big sister, in this and always my inspiration to do great things.*

Bethune visited the WANDs campsites and enthusiastically promoted the organization's efforts to secure positions for Negro women in the war effort. Based in Chicago, the WANDs opened its membership to any American girl or woman regardless of age. According to the WANDs brochure, it was a voluntary war service organization, the objectives of which were four-fold: give attention to women's participation in the war effort; encourage women to unite for an American victory; see that women are prepared to serve during the war effort; and work with government agencies. The brochure stated: "You must be willing to give voluntarily of your time in the program of the WANDs, and it is required that you recruit others in our service for victory." All members were trained in war work through classes and training. Brown appealed to women:

We, the WANDs, appeal to every American woman to get into the battle, and fight for American Security, and the future happiness of our children. Our Battle must be won, before Victory can be assured. Our men on the Front line are dependent upon our success on the Home Front. Womanpower of the Nation, must serve her country in every Capacity. In the Army, and Navy, as Nurses; on the Home Front—in industry and as volunteers. Not one single stone must be left unturned…Our Country is dependent upon its women, who are the Buyers of her nation, to save her from inflation. We as a group must be instrumental in securing the lasting peace we seek…Victory is our Goal—Freedom for all people of the world. Women of my race are loyal Americans.

The WANDs mission blended with Bethune's activities to secure positions for Negro women throughout the military support groups for women. In a WANDs newsletter, Bethune wrote:

The hour has come when women on the home front must give more of themselves in helping to win the war. Today, women in the four corners of America stand should to shoulder with men in this great struggle for a people's victory, and a people's peace...We will stand squarely back of the Army in its effort to perpetuate a true democracy for all the people, all over the world. I am encouraged by what our women have done and are doing in this war program...I heartily encourage you to join with using this national effort to utilize all of our energies and woman power in helping to obtain the extension of the four freedoms...There is no middle road today; either we win or lose, and I am sure that no woman will let it be said that her side lost because it felt the lack of her help, but rather, that her side won, because it felt the strong arm of its womanhood around it.

One newspaper account from February 24, 1945, reported:

The affair brought together women of many nationalities, races and creeds, which Bethune pointed out is one of the objectives of [NCNW]. Bethune stated: This building is dedicated to the united service of mankind where women of every race, creed and religion are welcome. It is only through our united efforts that we can hope to build a lasting peace." Madame Liataud, wife of Haitian Ambassador, paid tribute to the contributions of American women to the war effort... "We can do much in this connection to provide a firm basis for better understanding, love and tolerance among men." Madame Wei Tao-ming, wife of Chinese Ambassador[,] sent two representatives who brought greetings. "Human achievement knows no distinction of sex, race or creed, and benefits flowing from such achievement redound to the welfare of all the peoples throughout the world. It is my fervent hope that the shining examples of the honorees of the council will inspire us all to greatest efforts to bring about an early victory for our cause and the establishment of the just and durable peace."

The inaugural honor roll featured international women and exceptional coverage from the black press. Bethune reveled in the moment when women were able to celebrate each other as equals in the NCNW House. Her dream of breathing freely among accomplished women removed the ugliness of segregation for a moment. Her sentiments are reflected in the program, which stated, "Today when human values are so intimately tied in with the world-wide struggle for liberation, women are demonstrating in individual and group activities a sense of responsibility to their country and their times. [The NCNW] is privileged today to honor these representative American women, who are but a symbol of the mind the heart and soul of the womanhood of the world, who united work for a world of peace, freedom and justice for all."

Subsequent roll of honor winners broadened the spectrum of innovation within education, politics and culture. Bethune's realization of true democracy revolved around the honor roll receptions, and it established the NCNW as a clearinghouse qualified to recognize women trailblazers.

In 1946, NCNW established a committee and created criteria for the honor roll. The awards committee consisted of seven women: Vivian Carter Mason, Thomasina W. Johnson, Dr. Marion T. Wright, B. Beatrix Scott, Marion H. Elliot, Mrs. Clark Forman and Mame Mason Higgins. On January 24, meeting minutes reported the reason for the creation of the award: "The Council is concerned with bringing out women who have made outstanding achievements in their field of endeavor, and have made a contribution to a better understanding of racial groups." Initially, the criteria stated that only twelve women would be honored each year, but the committee believed that the number should be flexible to include more if necessary. The nine-point criteria included the following:

1. *Candidates should be chosen from the various fields or endeavor, such as Art, Literature, Science, Social Welfare, Human Relations, International Relations, etc.*
2. *Candidates shall be chosen who because of unusual meritorious performance in their occupation or profession rate public recognition of their achievement, regardless of race, color, creed or national origin.*
3. *Candidates shall be chosen whose achievements or activities constitute a contribution to a greater understanding of, appreciation for and acceptance of the Negro as a citizen.*
4. *Candidates shall be chosen whose activities are creative in character and have embraced and extended the base of human relationships.*
5. *Candidates shall be chosen who because of a position for which they are qualified have achieved distinction which is characterized by unusual responsibilities and duties.*

6. Selection of candidates shall be based on accumulated achievement and effort.

7. Twelve candidates shall be based on accumulated achievement and effort.

8. The proportional representation plan shall be used in making final selection of candidates.

9. Twelve candidates shall be named.

An undocumented aspect of the honor roll was an NCNW member honoree. Within each class of awardees, there was an NCNW member whose "unusual meritorious performance" advanced NCNW and the larger move toward civil rights. The committee involved other NCNW members in the process. On January 18, 1946, Higgins wrote Hilda Orr Fortune, asking:

> *Would you be good enough to get pertinent facts concerning the following three women who are in the New York community. You understand that none of these awards have been made, so get the information as quietly as you can. The names are: Selma Burke, Maida Springer and Judge Jane Bolin. We are especially anxious to have this data in the office by January 23 and I hope you will forgive me for such a rush order. But, as Mrs. Bethune says all the time when she talks about you, "Hilda will do it." Lots of luck.*

The 1946 honorees were: Charity Adams, Jane Bolin, Lois Mailou Jones, Pauli Murray, Virginia Durr, Eslanda Goode Robeson, Florence J. Harriman, Catherine Lealted, Arenia T. Mallory, Agnes Meyer, Maida Springer and Helen Gahagan Douglas. The 1946 program insert read, "Each is but a symbol of the character and quality of the service which the womanhood of America and the world is making to bring early fulfillment, rich and abundant living for all people." Charity Adams served in the Women's Army Auxiliary Corps (WACs). She served over the 6888th Central Postal Directory Battalion in Europe, delivering mail to nearly 7 million American troops. Her leadership boosted the morale of other black women serving in the military. During her military career, Adams fought for racial equality and personally challenged racism in various forms. She retired from the military as lieutenant colonel, the highest rank possible.

Jane Bolin was the first black female judge. She served in New York's Domestic Relations Court. She was also the first black woman to graduate from Yale Law School and the first black woman admitted to the New York bar. During her career, Judge Bolin advocated for the rights of juveniles. She viewed her position as an intermediary for troubled children in a country that viewed poverty and lack of opportunity as a precursor to criminal tendencies. Her advocacy for the youth broadened the scope of civil rights to include equality for children/young adults.

Lois Mailou Jones was a visual artist, educator, scholar, mentor and professor of art at Howard University. Jones's artistic work provided illustrations for NCNW, ASNLH and numerous other black publications.

In the early 1940s, Pauli Murray was a law student at Howard University, and her role as tactician and advisor to undergraduate activists during a sit-in demonstration of the Civil Rights Committee from 1943 to 1944 aided in desegregation of luncheon counters. She worked with the Urban League and the WPA's teachers program. In 1946, she served as the deputy attorney general for the Department of Justice in Sacramento, California. In response to being honored, Murray wrote, "I am overwhelmed with gratitude over the decision of your awards committee. Actually, I am but the instrument [of] hundreds of 'little people' whose kindnesses, whose dreams and aspirations are expressed through me. This award should go to them, and I will accept it on their behalf." Murray lived in California during 1946 and was unsure if her chronic health issues would preclude her from traveling. She arranged for her award to be accepted by her adopted mother, Mrs. Pauline F. Dame.

Virginia Durr, a white female activist, appealed to the awards committee because of her adherence to most every criterion listed. In 1933, she moved to Washington after her husband accepted a position with the Reconstruction Finance Corporation. It was in Washington that her activism began. She joined the Woman's National Democratic Club, and she became involved with the campaign to abolish the poll tax, which denied southern blacks and the poor the right to vote. In 1938, she and others founded the Southern Conference for Human Welfare (SCHW). The SCHW was a biracial coalition formed to challenge racial segregation and dedicated to improving living conditions in the South. In 1941, Durr became vice-president of the SCHW's evolving civil rights subcommittee, which eventually became the National Committee to Abolish the Poll Tax, with Durr as its vice-chair.

Eslanda Goode Robeson, wife of internationally acclaimed entertainer/activist Paul Robeson, was more than simply a housewife to the NCNW. Her professional life consisted of political activity and agency for African self-determination. In 1941, she co-founded the Council on African Affairs (CAA). The CAA consisted of black Americans who lobbied against any form of colonialism in Africa. Her intellect, writing ability and academic background provided her with the tools necessary to shed light on the detrimental effect of colonization on African people. She also served as a delegate observer for the fledgling United Nations in 1945.

Florence J. Harriman was the oldest woman honored. Born in 1870, she dedicated her life to social justice and equality even though she was a privileged white woman. Her father, a wealthy shipping magnate, ensured his children's success. She herself was a suffragist, socialite and organizer. In the 1940s, she served as the second woman appointed as a foreign minister to Norway. During her tenure as minister to Norway in World War II, she organized evacuation efforts while hiding in a forest from the Nazi invasion. She returned to the United States and continued her involvement in the Democratic Party, serving as chairwoman for the committee. She worked tirelessly for home rule and voting rights in the nation's capital. A Washington resident since 1920, she felt the sting of being denied the right to vote in national elections. Harriman lived during the time the District received no electoral votes, so she effectively could not vote in presidential elections for several decades. She did not allow her age, gender or political ideas to limit her influence or redirect her intentions.

Dr. Catharine D. Lealtad was the first black female graduate of Minnesota's Macalester College, where she earned a double major degree in chemistry and history in 1915 with highest honors. She taught for a year in Ohio and then moved to New York to work for the YWCA. Gifted and intelligent, she encountered numerous racist moments. This resulted in her traveling to Lyon, France, to study medicine. She received her medical degree from the University of Paris in 1933, specializing in pediatrics. In World War II, she was commissioned as a major in the U.S. Army, where she supervised medical services for displaced children. At the end of the war, she worked at Sydenham Hospital, the first voluntarily interracial hospital in New York.

Arenia T. Mallory was a school founder. She opened the Saints Industrial and Literary School as a private secondary school for children in Lexington, Mississippi. The Saints Industrial operated under the Church of God in Christ, a large black Pentecostal denomination. She advocated for civil rights and equality for the poor throughout Holmes County, Mississippi. Mallory blended her spirituality with her activism as an example of self-help.

• Awards to Twelve Outstanding Women of 1946 •

The twelve Women of the Year were cited at Council House on Friday, March 15th. Only two honorees, Judge Jane Bolin and Dr. Catherine Lealtad, were unable to be present. Reading from right to left: Mary McLeod Bethune, Virginia Foster Durr, Lois M. Jones, Charity Adams, Helen Gahagan Douglas, Maida S. Springer, Pauli Murray, Agnes Myer, Essie G. Robeson, Arenia C. Mallory, Daisy B. Harriman.

Aframerican Women's Journal article with the 1946 Roll of Honor awardees. *Courtesy Mary McLeod Bethune Council House, NPS.*

Agnes Meyer was the wife of Eugene Meyer, a multimillionaire and owner of the *Washington Post*. Agnes contributed critical articles to the *Post* about the New Deal. However, conditions during World War II domestically and abroad radicalized her. She wrote exposés about the economic problems facing migrant workers and black people. She lobbied for desegregation and human rights.

Maida Springer was a Panamanian-born labor activist. During the Depression, the working conditions of garment workers radicalized her, resulting in a life-long commitment to organizing labor for better wages and conditions. In 1945, Springer was the first Negro woman to represent American labor abroad. Government agencies promoted the exchange trip between Britain and the United States through the Office of War Information. Yvette Richards, author of *Maida Springer: Pan Africanist & International Labor Leader*, described the trip, saying, "The responsibilities included meeting with British women working in the war industries, exchanging experiences concerning war work conditions and discussing postwar plans." Springer was the first black woman selected to represent the American labor community internationally and demonstrated the gap between the ideal and lived realities within the labor movement. Larger issues of communism, anti-communism and colonization swirled around her, yet she seized the opportunity to promote equality for garment workers. The international delegation came to Washington in January 1945, but Springer was not allowed to stay in the Statler Hotel with the delegation of white women. She was lodged at the Council House.

> *Under ordinary circumstances, to have been invited to be the guest of Dr. Bethune was a great honor.* [But if] *I had known about the segregation I would face, I would never have gone to D.C. to be treated like that when I was going on an overseas trip for the Office of War Information! And I was selected* [as] *one of four people in the* [United States] *to go! Had I known that this might have been one of the conditions, no, I wouldn't have gone.*

Springer was angered that behind the scenes the government was tolerating segregation and exclusion while publicly heralding her appointment and using her as a symbol of racial progress. Refused taxi service and hotel accommodations, she was hotly incensed. However, after a phone call by Bethune, she was chauffeured in a limo to her meeting. Prior to leaving the Council House, this bitter experience provided Springer with a teaching moment from Bethune. She lectured gently on the larger opportunity to travel abroad, saying, "Learn about the conditions and problems and meet people and come back and report to the Council, report to my union and my colleagues." The mission was etched on Springer's heart and changed the trajectory of her intentions regarding labor organizing. Springer applauded Bethune's work to include all women.

Helen Gahagan Douglas was a starlet of the silver screen turned politician. Born into an educated and privileged family, Douglas was initially discouraged from an acting career by protective parents. However, her knack for theater attracted attention and led to a successful but short-lived career. The looming threat of World War II resulted in her joining thousands in the Anti-Nazi League. By 1937, Hollywood was politically awakening to the shifting climate. During this time, Douglas organized a Christmas party for migrant children that attracted thousands. After

British labor women visit the Council House in Washington, D.C. Also pictured is Maida Springer, seated in the center. *Courtesy Mary McLeod Bethune Council House, NPS.*

the party, she toured migrant camps and attended government hearings concerning citizen welfare. She joined John Steinbeck's Committee to Aid Agricultural Workers. She became chairman in 1939 and worked hard to publicize the needs of migrant laborers as well as push the public to demand labor laws. Also in 1939, she met Aubrey Williams of the NYA. This encounter resulted in the Douglas and Roosevelt families becoming fast friends and political allies. Douglas broadened her political position to include involvement in the Women's Division of the Democratic Party, bringing her closer to Eleanor Roosevelt. In 1944, she campaigned for Congress and was elected. Her campaign was frustrated by racism and red-baiting, but her win allowed her the opportunity to advocate for her constituents. In 1945, she arrived in Washington and focused her attention on housing shortages and racial equality. She viewed political issues as simply right or wrong, irrespective of race or gender. A liberal and advocate for the poor, she desired to be the voice of ordinary people. Her liberalism opened her to red-baiting attacks, which she shrugged off through a statement she dubbed "my credo." Her political advocacy sought to provide a strong economy, jobs and affordable housing for all American citizens. Her certificate celebrated her "superb statesmanship" as a freshman Congresswoman. Through Roosevelt, she met Bethune and hired a black secretary to demonstrate her commitment to jobs and racial equality.

In 1947, Marian Anderson headlined the honorees. Other recipients were Ingrid Bergman, Artemesia Bowden, Vijaya Pandit, Alma Illery, Mary C. Holliday, Helen Mills Scarborough, Georgianna Sibley, Venice T. Spraggs, Madeline Morgan Stratton and Sara Spencer Washington. In the *Aframerican Journal*, Anderson was eloquently described: "Like the truly great, the power of her personality is expressed through the dignity and simplicity of her life...a voice heard once in a hundred years." A black contralto and one of the most celebrated singers of her time, her singing career was spent performing in concert and recital. She did operatic arias. She was an important figure in the struggle for civil rights. When the DAR refused to allow her to sing to an integrated audience, the 1939 incident placed her into the spotlight of international activism. In response to her refusal, she performed an open-air concert on the steps of the Lincoln Memorial.

Ingrid Bergman's most enduring role came in 1942, when she played Ilsa in the wartime romance *Casablanca*. The film was a box office success, endearing her to fans for years to come. In 1946, she played Joan of Arc in the play *Joan of Lorraine*, to much acclaim. Bergman was selected for her stand against Washington managers who refused to seat Negroes in their theaters.

Artemesia Bowden was an educator who assumed the position of principal at St. Philip's Normal and Industrial School in Texas. The school was operated as an Episcopal day school for African American girls. During her tenure, she added a boarding department. By 1926, the school achieved private junior college status. She eventually served as president. During the Depression, the Episcopal Church withdrew its financial support from the school, but Bowden refused to concede to defeat. She campaigned to have the municipal district in San Antonio fund the school as it did white institutions. In 1942, the school district reluctantly incorporated St. Philip's.

Vijaya Pandit was an Indian diplomat and politician. She was the sister of Jawaharlal Nehru, former prime minister of India, and she was the first Indian woman to hold a cabinet post. In 1937, she was elected to the provincial legislature. She was appointed minister of local self-government and public health. In 1946, she was elected to the Constituent Assembly in

the United Provinces. After British colonization in 1947, she entered the diplomatic service and became Indian ambassador to the Soviet Union. She served two terms in British jails for her political beliefs. At the United Nations, she debated the abuse of Indians in South Africa. Her victories affected the welfare of all colonial areas and influenced Americans and the world.

Alma Illery founded Camp Achievement, using her wit and passion to create memorable experiences with nature for city youth. She raised chicks in her row house basement to provide eggs and meat for campers. Her interest in social work began in the 1930s when she witnessed poor hospital conditions for Negro patients. She recruited six friends and raised money for material to make sheets for patients. The Achievement Club was a service organization that grew to fifty chapters across the country. Like Bethune, Illery believed in the power of faith. She believed that God created everyone equal; however, prejudice was a learned behavior that required reprogramming and personal interactions to alleviate. The camp started on property donated by a white woman who sought to memorialize the Negro who saved her father's life many years earlier in an industrial accident.

Mary C. Holliday served as one of the five hundred Jeans County supervisors. A teachers' teacher, Holliday bridged the gap between accredited curricula into practical terms, while Helen Mills Scarborough, of Liberia, also made notable inroads in education. Scarborough sought to provide education to all children from elementary to high school.

Georgianna Sibley, a white woman, was known as a leader in the ecumenical movement. She fought for civil and human rights through bridging the world's gaps in trust and understanding through faith. She maintained a great interest in the Y movement and served on the national board of the YWCA.

Venice T. Spraggs served as the chief of the Chicago Defender's Washington Bureau. She was the first black member of Theta Sigma Phi, the professional fraternity for women in journalism.

Opposite, top: Mary McLeod Bethune presents the NCNW Roll of Honor certificate in 1947.

Opposite, bottom: Mrs. Bethune and recipients of the 1947 Roll of Honor award. *Courtesy Mary McLeod Bethune Council House, NPS.*

Madeline Morgan Stratton was an educator, historian and activist. She dedicated her career to raising awareness of black history through curriculum development for public education. In 1942, she successfully created the first black history curriculum in the Chicago Public Schools system. This accomplishment garnered national attention and propelled her to become an innovator in cultural education. Her "Supplementary Units for a Course in Social Studies" provided a rubric for teaching American history to diverse students. Her work was recognized by the State of Illinois. The Illinois General Assembly passed the House Bill 251 in 1945, resulting in all public schools incorporating Negro history in their curricula throughout the state.

Sara Spencer Washington opened the Arctic Avenue Beauty Salon in Atlantic City. She provided instruction in beauty through a door-to-door service that was accompanied by products for purchase and demonstration. She patented a hair curl remover. At the height of operation, her Apex Beauty Products manufactured more than seventy products sold by some forty-five thousand Apex agents nationwide. Washington became one of the earliest black female millionaires.

In 1948, NCNW honored eighteen women. These awardees were selected for a wide range of activities from civil rights to the arts to archives to nutrition. The honorees were Sadie T. Alexander, Carol Brice, Meta Warwick Fuller, Margaret Halsey, Flemmie P. Kittrell, Norma Boyd, Doris Ryer Nixon, Dorothy Porter, Mrs. Jessie Vann, Daisy George, M.E. Tilley, Ruth Weyand, Stella Counselbaum, Margaret Towns Haley, Sue Bailey Thurman, Helen Curtis and Cecelia Cabiness Saunders.

Sadie T. Alexander accomplished a number of firsts. In 1927, she became the first black woman admitted to the Pennsylvania Bar. She was the first black woman to earn a PhD in economics from Wharton and the first black person to hold both a PhD and a JD degree. In 1921, she was the first national president of the Delta Sigma Theta sorority. Her many firsts propelled her into national fame. The attention led her to craft a unique public persona. "Alexander offered herself as a new kind of race woman, one you would hire as an attorney or as an economist, as well as one you should admire for her brilliance." She understood the power of media in forming opinions, so she opted to employ constructive uses of the press to accentuate the possibilities dormant within black women. Her image was that of a consummate professional, tireless advocate and informed attorney. She served as an attorney for a number of black organizations, such as the African Methodist Church, Delta Sigma Theta and NCNW.

Mrs. Bethune presenting certificates to the 1947 Roll of Honor honorees. *Courtesy Mary McLeod Bethune Council House, NPS.*

Her training in social science fused with legal remediation, resulting in laws being changed throughout Philadelphia, her home city. She was appointed by President Truman to the Committee on Civil Rights, whose landmark publication, *To Secure These Rights*, was essential to Truman's desegregation of the military.

Carol Brice was a leading contralto. She was one of the first black classically trained singers to record extensively and the first black musician ever to win the prestigious Walter W. Naumburg Foundation Award. She sang in 1941 in honor of Franklin Delano Roosevelt's third inauguration.

Meta Warwick Fuller is one of the earliest black female sculptors. She studied in Paris with a number of artists, such as French sculptor Auguste Rodin. Her depictions of the African and African American experience were vivid.

Margaret Halsey was a writer. Her first book, *With Malice Towards Some* (1938), grew out of her experiences in Europe. Her controversial book

Mrs. Bethune presents Roll of Honor awards to Eleanor Daily and Carol Brice. *Courtesy Mary McLeod Bethune Council House, NPS.*

Color Blind: A White Woman Looks at the Negro openly attacked racism. Halsey plucked at the core fear of interracial sexuality and economic exploitation.

Flemmie P. Kittrell was the founding chair of the Department of Home Economics at Howard. She was the first black woman to earn a PhD in nutrition from Cornell University, in 1935. Her interest in women and children propelled her into international arenas. Through the field of home economics, she sought to heighten the quality of life for all people, regardless of nationality, creed or color. She desired to optimize the home experience for families, thereby elevating society to an artistic form of life that allowed everyone to operate at their fully realized potential. Aware of racial discrimination, she still believed in a God able to overcome and remove barriers. A Christian who ministered without a collar or pulpit, she used domestic science as a way of praising God and doing his work to properly feed women and children. She conducted a six-month nutrition study in Liberia. Her findings were published in a booklet titled "Preliminary Food and Nutrition Survey of Liberia under the auspices of the U.S. State Department." Through her research, she realized that a number of West African countries were experiencing "hidden hunger," a state of satiated malnourishment. Lack of meat protein contributed to this phenomenon. Through her training in nutrition, she was able to suggest dietary augmentation as well as industrial innovations to alleviate the problem. The success of her innovation opened doors to opportunities: winning a Fulbright Professorship to Baroda University in India. In a lecture, she stated:

> *The only way to live well in the world is first to live well in the family. Learn peace, love, understanding, forgiveness in home then one can live that way in the world...We want beauty in the home. God is beauty, love, intelligence, truth. How shall we teach all these things in connection with home economics? We need schools at all levels...Each person is basically intelligent but the intelligence of some has not been developed. When it is developed we may solve our own problems and think.*

Norma Boyd was one of sixteen founders of the Alpha Kappa Alpha sorority that began at Howard. Boyd worked as an educator in Washington public schools, and her interest in international affairs resulted in taking students to Congressional hearings. In 1938, she established the Non-Partisan Council (NPC). The NPC was among the first groups to represent black interests. In the 1940s, NPC lobbied for civil rights legislation as well as various government agencies to integrate their staffs.

111

Doris Nixon was a civic leader, particularly on the homefront during World War II. She became a national vice-president of the American Women's Voluntary Services (AWVS). Founded in 1940, the AWVS trained women to drive ambulances, fight fires and provide emergency medical assistance in anticipation of unexpected bombings.

Dorothy Porter worked at Howard for the Moorland Foundation. A bibliographer and curator, she innovated librarianship and grew the Howard collection. She served NCNW's library and archives initiative and was one of the first two black women to receive a master's in library science from Columbia University. She published bibliographies and articles to empower scholars and students to embrace historical sensitivity and to value their own stories.

Jessie Vann, widow of Robert Vann, crusaded for the *Pittsburgh Courier*. By World War II, the paper had a circulation of more than 250,000 and offices in fourteen cities. It published Eastern, Midwest and West Coast editions. Vann embraced her husband's vision and worked to have the *Courier* become a vehicle for black political empowerment and economic and cultural improvement. Although he did not live to see his dreams manifest, his vision drove the paper's agenda for social justice and civil rights. Articles that campaigned against lynching and for better education and employment paved the way for the reporting of larger civil rights challenges and firmly placed the black press at the helm of documenting and exposing injustice. By 1948, the paper grew to its greatest circulation of 450,000 issues. The advocacy of the paper pressed President Truman to integrate the armed forces.

Daisy George was a member of Iota Phi Lambda sorority, an affiliate of the NCNW. The Iotas were a professional and business sorority with international membership. Ms. George was the founder of the Northeast Bronx Day Care Center. She dedicated her career to childcare and development and training of young people. Her work with children and skills training reinforced the mission of the NCNW. Her innovations in stemming the tide of high school dropouts alleviated prospective unemployment rolls. This endeavour added skilled and patriotic citizens to the labor force.

Mrs. M.E. Tilley was a notable Methodist church member who served on the forefront of better race relations throughout the south. The *Aframerican Journal* reported, "She has stood for everything that is fair and just for all peoples. She has been a great builder of better race relations and has been a fearless and courageous leader among women, both politically and socially." Tilley's crusade for civil rights was monumental for southern womanhood imbued with spiritual fortitude.

Mrs. Bethune presents the Roll of Honor certificate to Daisy George. *Courtesy Mary McLeod Bethune Council House, NPS.*

Ruth Weyand was fêted for her hard work in helping to outlaw court enforcement of racially restrictive covenants in housing. A restrictive covenant blocked select people from purchasing private property. Many neighbors signed "unofficial" agreements to keep their neighborhood white, which effectively and illegally restricted the ability of blacks to purchase housing regardless of their ability to pay for the property.

Stella Counselbaum contributed to the formation of archives and assisted with NCNW's effort. Margaret Towns Haley provided social services for less fortunate people. Sue Bailey Thurman was an NCNW darling. Her selflessness in offering to serve as the founding editor of the *Aframerican Journal*, as well as spearheading the archives and library project, did not stop when she and her husband relocated to California. Thurman continued to advocate for the preservation of important materials and also challenged women to find their voice within the political and economic arenas.

Helen Curtis served as a missionary to Liberia with her husband, James L. Curtis. James was appointed by President Woodrow Wilson as U.S. Minister to Liberia, and Curtis traveled with her husband, earning the moniker "Mistress of the American Legation at Monrovia." In 1918, she was sent to Europe as the first Negro woman YWCA executive. There she supervised the reburial of U.S. dead at the largest American cemetery in Remagen, Germany. During World War II, she operated a canteen for soldiers in Brooklyn and served as the vice-president of the Harlem YWCA. Her life of service to military personnel and their families reflected NCNW's mission.

Cecelia Cabaniss Saunders was a graduate of Fisk University and Tuskegee Institute, where she received her master's of social science. After a period of teaching at South Carolina State University, she assumed the position of executive director of the Upper Manhattan YWCA. She remained with the YWCA over thirty years. During her tenure, she raised the funds needed to expand the Y from a simple residence to a million-dollar facility. She sought to help humanity through building an organization where untrained Negro women could gain beneficial training and experience.

The 1948 honorees were equally accomplished. The *Aframerican Journal* reported, "The fifteen women [are] a symbol of the mind, the heart and the soul of womenhood of the world who unitedly work for a world of peace, freedom and justice for all." One of these women, Ethel J. Alpenfels, a noted anthropologist, taught children how to interpret scientific aspects of racial

Mrs. Bethune presenting Roll of Honor certificate to Mrs. Helen Curtis. *Courtesy Mary McLeod Bethune Council House, NPS.*

differences. Her study was a part of the Bureau for Intercultural Education in 1944. She sought to express the depth of cultural differences as complex and beautiful.

Frances Bolton was a state representative from Ohio. She was active in public health, nursing education and other social service, education and philanthropic work. She was elected as a Republican by special election, in 1940, to fill the vacancy caused by the death of her husband, Chester C. Bolton. She was subsequently reelected to succeeding terms until the 1960s. Her passion for nursing, education and public health mirrored NCNW interests.

Charlotte Hawkins Brown was an educator whose access to good schools impelled her to share the ability to learn with other black people. Prior to opening her own school, she took courses in education. In 1902, she founded the Freeman Palmer Memorial Institute with initial assistance from the American Missionary Association (AMA) in Sedalia, North Carolina. She modeled her school after Booker T. Washington's Tuskegee Institute. During the school's first year, she purchased clothing and school supplies for her students. A short time after her arrival, the AMA decided to close several schools, including Brown's. She remained committed to Palmer Memorial. Moreover, people in the community appreciated her being there and supplemented the school's needs by donating land. In 1946, the school's facilities were valued at nearly $600,000. Brown was an active member in the club movement. She was a founding member of NCNW and a close friend of Bethune. She viewed her role as educator in the tradition of racial uplift. Her career mirrored Bethune. She assisted in organizing the North Carolina State Federation of Negro Women's Clubs (NCFNW), which served as an umbrella organization. The NCFNW opened a home for delinquent Negro girls and persuaded the state to improve economic conditions of rural Negroes with job opportunities. Similar to Bethune, she assisted in directing funds from federal and state agencies to needy communities in North Carolina.

Alice Coachman was the first black female athlete to win an Olympic gold medal. She was also the first American woman to win an Olympic medal in track and field. During her prime athletic years, the 1940 and 1944 Olympic games were cancelled because of World War II, but in 1948, she competed. At the age of twenty-five and suffering from back troubles, she set an Olympic record before eighty-three thousand people in the high jump with a leap over five feet high. Her record stood for eight years.

Eleanor Curtis Dailey was the fourth vice-president of NCNW and director of Region Five. She was a civic and social leader well known for her promotion of intercultural and international goodwill. Christine Ray Davis served as the chief clerk for the Committee on Expenditures in the executive branch of the House, and she was honored for her twelve years of "meritorious service" as a secretary. She served two Illinois congressmen, Arthur W. Mitchell and William L. Dawson. Martha Elliot served in international relations as the assistant director general of the World Health Organization. She was selected for her work in international health. The *Aframerican Journal* reported, "Dr. Elliot is [closely] allied to [the NCNW] through her work in maternal and child health. In 1948 [she was] presented with the Lasker Award for her direction of wartime maternity and infant care programs for infants and wives of GI's."

Rosa Slade Gragg was a civic leader who contributed to educational, social and political arenas. She founded the Slade-Gragg Academy of Practical Arts in 1947, the first black vocational school in Detroit. She modeled her school after Tuskegee. The school trained over two thousand women and returning veterans. Beyond the job training, she established a youth center, library and archives for Bethel AME Church. Gragg fostered better relations between blacks and whites by lecturing and breaking down barriers. Ella Griffin served as editorial assistant for the U.S. Department of Education and was fêted for her contributions to adult education. She emphasized literacy. During the reception, Griffin announced plans to travel to Haiti to replicate her work in adult literacy. Frieda Miller was the Chief of the Women's Bureau in the U.S. Department of Labor and a longtime friend of the NCNW. She was celebrated for her achievements in international fields of human and labor relations.

Cornelia Otis Skinner was an American author and actress. She appeared in several plays before embarking on a tour of the United States from 1926 to 1929 in a one-woman performance of short character sketches she wrote herself. Skinner fought for and promoted human rights and freedom of opportunity for all to enjoy in the theater. Chase Going Woodhouse was a representative from Connecticut who served as a consultant to the National Roster of Scientific and Specialized Personnel, War Manpower Commission 1942–1944. She was honored for her leadership in organizing women and her contributions to social progress. Marjorie Stewart Joyner was an employee of Madame C.J. Walker. She invented and patented a permanent wave machine that curled hair for extended periods of time. She was the founder and president of the National Beauty Culturist League of America

Mrs. Bethune with Roll of Honor winners. *Courtesy Mary McLeod Bethune Council House, NPS.*

in 1945. Her entrepreneurial skills empowered other women. Her emphasis on beauty culture provided black women with self-made definitions and images of natural beauty. She contributed to expanding opportunities for youth through civic and cultural activities.

Muriel Rahn was a singer and actress. Prior to her entertainment career, she taught in public schools. In 1942, she became the first black singer to perform in an opera at Carnegie Hall. Similar to the experience of other singers, she was barred from performing at the Ford's Theater in Baltimore because of segregated seating. She performed in front of segregated audiences and during her intermissions joined the picket line throughout the production. Her willingness to fight injustices was not limited to the Baltimore incident. She was a popular advocate for the fair treatment of black performers, often confronting theater producers and owners about their unjust treatment of blacks, forcing them to honor contracts that demoralized their humanity. She was honored for unselfish devotion to community projects throughout America.

Julia West Hamilton was the president of the Phyllis Wheatley YWCA. Hamilton was a pious woman who viewed her service to mankind as a divine calling. One article wrote, "[She] was one of God's best servants of this century, a woman of remarkably candid and clear intelligence, compassion and convictions that we are mere servants of Christ working together towards a common end." She was affectionately called "Mother of the District," serving the community for over forty years. She was an active member of the Metropolitan AME church. Another article called her the crusader who "possessed the Midas touch in community service in that everything in which she took an interest increased in spiritual value."

The Roll of Honor receptions firmly established NCNW as a leading organization of Negro women in particular and womanhood in general. The press coverage and attendees revealed a broad spectrum of social justice issues that women confronted, from health care to employment. The awards also celebrated the accomplishment of female "firsts" in athletics, politics, education and industry. Bethune realized aspects of her grand vision for the national headquarters. She welcomed familiar and inquisitive, domestic and foreign born to her home—the national home of contemporary Negro women. In that space, Negro women breathed free, unsegregated air, and they wore furs and gowns, drank from bone china and served tea from sterling silver sets. These trappings of middle-class living honored enslaved foremothers, acknowledged attainment of contemporary women and encouraged young women to dream bigger than their mothers. These opportunities were living epistles read through photographs, newspaper articles, soirees and parties, all of which Bethune employed to recast the Negro woman as a citizen, patriot and lady—one whose education, exposure and cultural relevance embraced being proud Negro women prepared to face the future as qualified equals.

ALL THE WORLD'S WELCOME:
INTERNATIONAL VISITORS

Throughout the 1940s, Bethune received a variety of international visitors. Men and women from Haiti, India, Britain and Liberia were welcomed to receptions and purposeful visits to the Council House. Bethune believed that discrimination was due in part to ignorance about a particular people; therefore, NCNW's house, archives and publications all worked to reintroduce Negro womanhood to the world. The Building Better Race Relations conference involved a variety of women's organizations of

Christians, Jews, trade unions and others. The principles of the meeting were demonstrated through the various international guests entertained at the House. The principles were:

> *Human equality is one of the foundation stones of our Republic. The pursuit of truth and the worship of God in freedom of conscience are inseparable from the American way of life. The duty to serve democracy and the right to enjoy its blessings and privileges are the essence of American citizenship. These principles must endure if the Nation is to survive. Neither self-regarding pride nor privilege must be allowed to undermine or corrupt the ideals that have made our country great. We hold that these great moral truths, above all things, can preserve our national unity...To the extent that America means racial understanding, religious freedom and equality of opportunity, America will measure up to her glorious past, her solemn present and her great future.*

The women agreed with Bethune about a better America where peace and equality would win the day. In the *Aframerican Journal*, an article titled "A People's Section for the United Nations" implored NCNW membership to learn about the function and possibilities for citizen women in the UN.

> *Understanding comes first and then action based on knowledge. Such is the credo of the Peoples Section for the* [UN] *which seeks to develop informed public opinion on* [UN] *issues...The Peoples Section has sprouted since its formation in January 1947 in 47 states, encompassing groups and individuals. It is on the road to serving as a channel of communication between the people of this country and the State Department, US officials* [and] *UN officials...The Peoples Section provides an answer* [on how to get involved] *because every member can become a force—an expression of opinion on matters facing* [international organizations].

Bethune and NCNW were invited participants at the Dumbarton Oaks Conference, which contributed to the formation of the UN. Moreover, NCNW was the only organization allowed to participate as an observer during the meetings. The Dumbarton Oaks Conference was held in 1944 in Washington's Georgetown neighborhood. The principal objective was to discuss the possibilities of creating an international organization that would maintain world peace in the wake of World War II. The Georgetown mansion received representatives from China, the Soviet Union, the United Kingdom and United States. This was the first step in the twentieth century since the League of Nations to promote an international organization concerned with peace. The conference's success needed a unilateral agreement; unfortunately, it did not directly happen. The disagreements among the attendees surrounded the voting system of the proposed Security Council and the membership requirements.

In 1945 at the Yalta Conference, lingering questions were resolved, resulting in the basis of negotiations for the San Francisco Conference, leading to the formation of the United Nations. Delegates from Haiti, India, Ethiopia and Liberia attended, as well as those from a number of Latin American countries. While no black American organizations attended the 1945 meeting, Walter White, secretary of the NAACP; W.E.B. Du Bois, the NAACP's director of special research; and Mary McLeod Bethune, of the National Council of Negro Women vis-à-vis the U.S. State Department, were present as observers. In conjunction with racial equity, Bethune pressed for the rights of women of all races. The sudden death of President Roosevelt reduced the influence black leadership had within the fledgling UN. For black America, the UN seemed to be an organization that allowed oppressed and marginalized people a chance to link issues of social injustice together globally. Clearly, black Americans advocated for themselves and addressed injustice, but the time was ripe to propel Bethune and the NCNW into the UN's world. With influential assistance from Eleanor Roosevelt, the NCNW was given participant observer status to future meetings of the UN. The protection of racial, ethnic and religious minorities occupied early discussions at the UN, which melded with the NCNW agenda.

Bethune issued a response to the National Negro Press Association about the meeting in San Francisco. In the *Atlanta Daily World* of May 1, 1945, she expressed a particular interest in the darker peoples of the world.

The Negro in America has an unprecedented opportunity [to] *parley on World Security to encompass a world view of the problems of peace, and to think in unison with the representatives of forty-six nations on the most effective means of settling national differences, of adjudicating all national and international grievances justly and equitably. This opportunity challenges the Negro not only to broaden his personal point of view, but to establish on a firmer basis, the elevation of his own status in America. Through this Conference, the Negro becomes closely allied with all the darker races of the world but more importantly he becomes integrated into the structure of the peace and freedom of all people everywhere. I am particularly interested in the trend of thought of the darker peoples of the world who are no longer a numerical minority.*

There were serious questions the Conference needed to address, such as colonialism, equality and autonomy. Black Americans organized to confront injustice, and in 1945, the National Negro Congress (NNC) drafted a petition to the United Nations to end racial discrimination in America. Bethune's participation in the NNC impelled her to remain vigilant in international decisions that impacted the lives of women in the postwar period. The NNC was an outgrowth of a conference organized at Howard in 1935. The conference sought to examine the conditions of Negro life in America. The scholars in economics, history, law, philosophy, sociology and other fields produced a stark portrait of Negro life with a hope-infused reality. Early members believed that the NNC would be an interclass movement that would dismantle segregation. Well-intentioned but faced with increasing suspicions of its being a communist group, the NNC was unable to survive. Concurrently, international events convulsed with struggles between justice and injustice throughout the world. The bittersweet reality of the UN mirrored hypocritical patterns of piecemeal equality. For example, its failure to acknowledge a racial and national equality clause introduced by the Chinese government signaled a level of ethnocentrism within this new global organization.

Still Bethune plodded along her course of turning the tide of discrimination through personal encounters. Bethune, like many other blacks, was fascinated with the formation of Haiti and Liberia. These two independent Negro nations provided successful models for Negro autonomy. Bethune called Haiti a symbol of attainable freedom. Prior to her 1949 visit to Haiti, she wrote in her *Chicago Defender* column:

Opposite, top: Reception honoring Ambassador Charles of Haiti and Minster King of Liberia. *From left to right:* Mrs. Bernice G. McIntosh (Instruction Supervisor, H.U. School of Social Work); Mrs. Marie Wilson; Mrs. Katherine F. Lenroot (Chief, Children's Bureau); and Mrs. Annie Lee Dav. *Courtesy Mary McLeod Bethune Council House, NPS.*

Opposite, botton: Visitors from Haiti at the Council House in Washington, D.C. *Courtesy Mary McLeod Bethune Council House, NPS.*

The prospect thrills me. Ever since L'Ouverture, fought the good fight to prevent reestablishment of slavery in Haiti [more than 150 years earlier], the island Republic has been a spiritual haven to the oppressed of African descent. She has been a symbol of freedom to those beyond her shores, who possibly, have met with material success, but have been spiritually frustrated by the barriers of citizenship...I shall be talking with the people of Haiti. I want to counsel with her women—the great spiritual resource of any nation, to try to broaden the circle of women's relationships. I want to talk with the young artists who are making the world conscious of their country with paint and canvas. I want to talk with elder statesmen and see Haiti, the beautiful still-to-be-developed republic through their eyes...I want to help strengthen the fraternal bonds between this island country and [America]. There is much that each can teach the other.

In 1949, Bethune was decorated by the Haitian government with the Order of Honor and Merit of the Republic of Haiti. She was the first woman to ever receive this prestigious award. The decoration was given to her in a ceremony attended by a distinguished gathering of teachers, friends and government officials. During her visit, she met with writers and artists and toured orphanages, hospitals and schools. She demonstrated concern for women's suffrage and nudged the government to extend voting rights to all citizens. She also rebuked Haitian people for internal discrimination between blacks and mulattoes. She wrote, "Women astute enough to drive a hard bargain in the [marketplace], are astute enough to drive another at the poll! We must help [Haitian people] to [break down] their own self-defeating prejudices exactly as we must [break down] ours in this country. No people can make progress...by hating, distrusting or suppressing each other." Also in 1949 she was decorated the Commander of the Order of the Star of Africa during the inauguration of Liberian president William Tubman. She traveled as a U.S. representative to Liberia. Her Liberia excursion was a "dream manifested" from her earlier desire to be a missionary in Africa.

Opposite, top: A reception at the Council House honoring Ambassador Charles of Haiti and Minister King of Liberia. *Courtesy Mary McLeod Bethune Council House, NPS*

Opposite, bottom: Tea honoring Ambassador Charles of Haiti and Minister King of Liberia. *From left to right:* Harriet West, Sarah King, Mr. and Mrs. Bunche and Katherine Hurley. *Courtesy Mary McLeod Bethune Council House, NPS.*

In Washington, NCNW hosted a reception honoring Ambassador of Haiti Joseph D. Charles and Liberian Minister Charles B. King and his wife at the Council House. The reception aimed to strengthen the historic relationships between the United States and the two independent republics. Over five hundred people attended, representing the governments of France, Denmark, India and Syria. Bethune said the reception was more than a social affair. One article quoted Bethune as saying, "If world peace is to be achieved, it becomes mandatory that all races, colors and creeds of people must know each other better in order that they may understand each other's problems and respect each other's hopes and aspirations. Here in a hotbed of international relationships we as citizens of a leading world power have a special responsibility to begin to build a bridge to peace through understanding."

The honorees were moved by the sincerity of Bethune's words. The receiving line was assisted by Howard's historian Dr. Rayford Logan, Venice T. Spraggs of the chief Washington bureau of the *Chicago Defender* and others. Seventy-five notable Washington women assisted in sponsoring the event, representing Howard, NCNW and other groups. During the course of the evening, Madame Lillian Evanti and Camille Nickerson furnished musical entertainment. The reception also formed the core of a new vision for Bethune. It served as a model for intercultural and educational programs for international women living in Washington as well as augmented NCNW's interracial programs.

Bethune reached out to international college students, seeding the intercultural collaboration in future leaders. In her *Chicago Defender* column, she mentioned the visit of two Indian women in the autumn of 1949. For one week, Svati Puwaiah, a nurse studying administration at Columbia University, and Lakshmi Rao, a doctoral student in biology at the University of Toronto, were Council House guests. The women were part of a delegation from the World Student Federation conference in Baltimore. About their visit, Bethune wrote:

> *Such interesting young women! They did not appear to regard their accomplishments as in any way remarkable or out of the ordinary, which might surprise some Americans who still hold a rather stereotyped picture of the restrictions experienced by Indian women…It was difficult to say who asked more questions—we or they! We were all getting such a fresh, new vision from our association with each other. I was reminded of Mahatma Ghandi [sic]…It seemed to me that I could sense the*

Faiz El-Kouri, Syrian ambassador, and his daughter at the Council House in Washington, D.C. *Courtesy Mary McLeod Bethune Council House, NPS.*

Mrs. Bethune at intercultural party for foreign students in 1948. *Courtesy Mary McLeod Bethune Council House, NPS.*

Indian visitors at the Council House in Washington, D.C. *From left to right:* Mrs. D. Chanduri, Mrs. R. Grewal, Mrs. T.S. Ram and Mrs. S.G. Singh. *Courtesy Mary McLeod Bethune Council House, NPS.*

heartbeat, the pulsation of yearning for light and for the opportunity for greater service, which seemed to surround these sisters from other lands…I am happy that I am alive, today. I look forward, each day, to the new contacts, the new impressions, the new experiences, the deepened understanding that come as I listen and learn from my fellow men and women of the world. I rejoice to realize the strides that we have made in dispelling hate and implanting deeply in all hearts, the spirit of love that must finally bring justice and peace and unity to us all.

WE SERVE AMERICA, KEEP YOUR JOB, YOUNG WOMEN AND EMPLOYMENT

In the wake of the Depression and in the throes of World War II, employment for black people was an essential part of the NCNW's advocacy for human rights. Bethune desired a livable wage and clean and honorable work for young people. Her work with the NYA afforded her the opportunity to see the hardship that poverty, rural living and racial discrimination inflicted on young people seeking to find employment to provide for themselves or their families. To level the playing field, NCNW instituted Keep Your Job clinics. In an article titled "Job Security and Negro Women," published in the May 1944 *Congress Vue*, Bethune expressed her concern for future job security regarding Negro women. In the wake of the creation of the NCNW's Employment Institute, plans were formulated for Hold Your Job clinics in industrial areas. The recommendations included involving community organizations, creating new labor-management relationships, reporting achievements of accomplished workers and stimulating the Negro woman worker through empowerment. Bethune wrote: "The awakening Negro woman recognizes that she can take her place in American life only by joining hands with all citizens who are dedicated to fight for democracy."

NCNW's main emphasis in 1944 included full employment, full citizenship exemplified through registration and voting and interracial goodwill. The imbalance in employment compelled NCNW to respond and assist young women in developing skills and finding lasting employment during and after the war. By 1946, Bethune fought for social security for older female workers. In a memo to NCNW leadership, she wrote:

Because of our collective interest in the job security of all the people in the post war period, and because [of] our particular interest in guaranteeing to Negro men and women the fullest protection in periods of unemployment, [NCNW] calls upon each organized group to support the following recommendations for Social Security.

1. Extension of un-employment insurance coverage to all employees.

2. Coverage of all gainful workers, including agricultural and domestic employees, public employees and self-employed persons including farmers.

3. Benefits during periods of extended or permanent disability like those for old-age retirement.

4. Increase in benefit amounts, particularly for low-paid workers.

The security of the Negro worker must be assured!

One incarnation of this program was a jobs security soiree held in May 1945, over which Muriel M. Alexander of Washington presided. The program included a tribute to mothers by Valera Rogers; remarks from Susie Elliott Dean of Women from Howard; student presentations; a musical selection, "Songs My Mother Taught Me," performed by Inita Kirtley; and a skit called "Down Payment on a Job," performed by five women under the direction of Evelyn Rink. There was an "On the Job" fashion show presented courtesy of Wal-Thom Tailors. A session called "Your Face: A Selling Point" included a cosmetic and hygiene demonstration by J.R. Watkins company. Hilda Orr Fortune, a personnel counselor with the Wright Aeronautical Corporation of Patterson, New Jersey, provided the keynote and spoke on "A Glimpse into the World of Work," providing examples of real world experiences the young women would encounter. Many of the program participants were NCNW-affiliated women infused with the vision of preparing young women for work while providing them access to a network of established professionals. Reaching across the chasm of formally educated and high school graduate women, Bethune desired to create a grand sisterhood of women, irrespective of one's field of work or education.

In May 1945 on WINX radio, the NCNW and the Women's Organization of Howard presented five female students who were preparing themselves for important, useful vocational service in the postwar world. The broadcast initiated a week designated by Howard and NCNW "as a period for considering vocational training and job opportunities." Traditional roles of teaching and clerical work were giving way to increasing opportunities in commercial arts, social work, law and engineering. The broadcaster noted, "Women are in increasing numbers breaking traditional occupational patterns, and are preparing themselves for significant posts in fields hitherto uninvaded by women as well as in fields into which relatively few women have ventured." Bernice Hammond was a commercial art student. She took classes in designing, sketching, theory, modeling, water color and linoleum block design. Hammond stated:

> *The Artist, though he is an individual creator, can contribute a great deal both to his community and to the world at large. After all, Art is a universal language—its fundamentals are understood by all people, in a common bond of understanding and friendship. A picture—whether it be a poster, or an extremely academic piece—may do more to bring about good will and understanding between groups of people or future nations of people, than a long treatise. As vehicles for expression and instruction, cartoons, illustrations, diagrams, models, murals, pictures are all excellent. The artist of tomorrow will be just as much of a politician or good will crusader as his fellow craftsman the writer.*

Another student, Mary Graves, sought a career in medical social work. The medical social worker, Graves explained, worked:

> *In hospitals* [dealing] *directly with the patients; as consultants they may be in Public Assistance Agencies where field workers come to her for help in securing adequate medical care for sick clients. Or a medical social worker might be allied with one of the Federal Agencies—the Children's Bureau or Social Security Board, for example, and if she were, she would no doubt travel to designated sections of the country giving advice to state and local health departments. The medical social worker is of most help to those patients whose illness is intensified by factors of a non-physical nature either within themselves or outside in their various environments. With returning veterans, many of whom will* [be] *shock victims, the medical social worker will find her responsibilities heavily increased.*

Margaret Gill pursued a career in law. When asked to explain the social benefits of this career path, Gill stated:

> *After every great war there comes a wave of crime—already we have had serious juvenile delinquency problems as well as innumerable adult crimes. Somehow, we believe that women lawyers will be in a particularly strategic*

International soiree at the YWCA. *From left to right:* Olga Margolin, Lynette Grittoes, Mary Church Terrell, Jeanetta Welch Brown and Chris Prouty Rosenfeld. *Courtesy Mary McLeod Bethune Council House, NPS.*

position—women are notably patient, tolerant, and understanding. A woman legally trained should be an excellent person to cope with the many taxing cases that will be the logical outgrowth of this world confusion. Perhaps we cannot all be as wise as Portia, but we believe that legal knowledge imposed on traditional womanly virtues will give women lawyers a distinctly useful place in the coming year. It will take understanding as well as wisdom to adjust the many problems of war marriages, precedence in job-placement, pensions, disability compensations, and [interpretating] the G.I. rights. As a prospective lawyer, I look forward to a great deal of hard, but useful work.

The students clearly presented their interests and developments within various professions. The radio broadcast heard throughout the city reinforced the black women's commitment to improving employability and contributing to building the postwar economy.

NCNW's We Serve America Week sought to highlight the accomplishments of Negro women in the war effort. In 1943, journalist Rebecca Stiles Taylor of the *Chicago Defender* acknowledged the NCNW's We Serve event, writing, "Today when women must of necessity play an important role in helping to safeguard the principles of democracy, the Negro woman naturally focuses her attention upon her role as a participant in this world-wide movement." The *Aframerican Journal* implored the membership to consider one of fifteen suggested projects to perform locally. The activities ranged from buying and selling war bonds, observing Bethune's birthday by collecting a dollar in tribute to her vision of the NCNW, producing and publishing a list of achievements by Negro women in their locale, hosting a roundtable or sponsoring a tea highlighting Negro women's accomplishments. *Aframerican* suggested hosting voter registration tables and offering foreign language classes to aid in communicating with other women of color. Finally, the *Aframerican* suggested a dime drive in which each member donated a dime and the total collection was donated to NCNW's headquarters. The article closed by saying, "Yours is the responsibility to keep alive the vision and aspirations of courageous women!"

CHAPTER 4

For the House

HOME RUNS, BROTHERLY LOVE AND BETHUNE BENEFIT GAMES

In recounting a 1925 baseball game, *Washington Daily American* newspaper editor Eugene Davidson described the atmosphere of Griffith Stadium:

> *The world series so far as Washington is concerned is over. Griffith Baseball Park, yesterday a human volcano of howling fans today is as quiet as the proverbial tombstone…for a home run does a bit more than thrill a yelping crowd. It eradicates entirely the handicap of color and makes the world more as the Divine Creator fashioned it. Colored man sat beside white man and discussed with each other the pros and cons of each play. Black and white man arose with a single urge as the flying sphere sailed from the bat of a player to register for the team a home run. White man slapped black man on the back and the cheers of both mingled with the yells of thousands, black and white…A single home run had made the whole world kin.*

Baseball, along with movies, drew large crowds from 1900 to 1950. Night games and Sunday afternoon doubleheaders were not only sporting events but also social outings. Women dressed up, and men wore suits and hats. Entire families spent their afternoons out at the games. Absences were noted when people were traveling or ill. World War II was a boom time for Negro leagues. The migration to war work increased urban populations and disposable income. Moreover, gas rations limited travel, and people stayed home instead of traveling to the seashore.

During the 1940s, life in Washington was invigorating and exciting but ultimately harrowing. The specter of segregation lingered in schools, restaurants and recreation. The all-American pastime of baseball was a victim of the age. On the other hand, Washington bustled with activity, and although the war preoccupied the capital city, Americans found reprieve in watching their favorite teams. For Negro Washington, the relocated Homestead Grays played in Griffith Stadium, attracting crowds and becoming an institution within the community. The Grays were originally from Pennsylvania and featured Negro League notables such as Josh Gibson, Buck Leonard, "Cool Papa" Bell and others.

For many, the 1940s Grays were possibly the greatest professional ball club ever assembled, regardless of race. The jewel in the Grays' crown was Josh Gibson. He had a strong arm and could slug the ball out of most parks. According to Buck O'Neil, famed first baseman and manager of the Kansas City Monarchs, who played against Gibson, "He was the best hitter I've ever seen. He would have rewritten the record book for homers had he played in the majors. He was our Babe Ruth." Washington fans had the privilege of seeing Gibson play for much of the decade before he died unexpectedly in 1947 at the age of thirty-six. In a ten-year period from 1938 to 1948, the Grays won nine league championships. Griffith Stadium was sometimes called the Washington Baseball Club Park, and from 1891 on, it hosted thousands of professional baseball games for over sixty years. It became known as Griffith Stadium in 1920 when Clark Griffith purchased a home for the Washington Senators.

Originating in Homestead, Pennsylvania, members of the famous Homestead Grays got their start playing ball. Early players were black steel mill workers who used the game to foster fellowship and unwind. Ensconced in the Negro community of Pittsburgh's Hill District, the team was without a field by 1938 with the demolition of Greenlee Field. With the loss of the field and a dwindling fan base, team owner Cumberland Willis Posey Jr. looked for a solution to save his team. Posey's business acumen possibly came from his father, Cumberland "Cap" Willis Posey Sr., owner of the Diamond Coke and Coal Company. He searched for a new home and found one in Washington's Griffith Stadium. Located at the corners of Seventh and Florida Avenues, it was directly in the heart of black Washington. Moreover, the number of potential fans was triple the size of Pittsburgh. Many black Pittsburghers disapproved of the move, and Posey conceded to allow the Grays to begin playing their Saturday home games at Forbes Field in Pittsburgh and their Sunday home games in Washington at Griffith Stadium.

The 1940–1941 seasons in Washington were not spectacular, even with the powerful playing of Josh Gibson and Buck Leonard. Gibson was dubbed the "Black Babe Ruth," while Buck Leonard's moniker was the "Lou Gehrig of black baseball." Initially, black Washingtonians were loyal to the Washington Senators. When World War II pulled players to military duty, it also changed the local population. The change worked in favor of the Grays and boosted their popularity. Throughout the war years, talk of integration threatened the Negro Leagues. Posey was anti-integration. He believed that integration signaled the end of Negro Leagues Baseball and ultimately the end of a form of black business. Joe Sewall wrote in the *Washington Tribune* in 1942:

> *When we say Negro baseball—we say Negro business, and big boy business. In no other phase of business have we anything that can compare, outside of a few insurances, with organized Negro baseball operating in several cities. To support [integration] is putting money out of our pockets back into race coffers that hire colored throughout and not at nickel and dime salaries…The plight of Negro baseball would be appalling to even imagine if the various club owners had to depend on our lettered Negroes to come out and support an effort that has reached a point where the type and brand of baseball the Negro teams are playing is on par with most of the big league teams…[T]he truck drivers, barbers, numbers players, janitors and street workers are supporting to keep an organized league alive.*

Posey's prediction came true when Jackie Robinson became the first black major league player for the Brooklyn Dodgers in 1947. Posey had died a year before, in March 1946, and the Grays disbanded in 1950. For a team with two homes, sportswriter Wendell Smith wrote, "Not only are the Grays champions of Negro baseball, but they are a cocky bunch of ballplayers. They do not believe that any team can beat them. They don't give a hoot for umpires, fans, newspaper men or anything else. Baseball is all they care about—it is their life."

NCNW utilized the popularity of baseball to sponsor a war bond rally in July 1944 prior to a game between the Brooklyn Bushwicks and the Grays. The NCNW membership was trisected into three teams: red, white and blue. Each team had a leader, captains and workers who were responsible for selling tickets. The biggest ticket seller won a prize. It was suggested that members become telephone bees who buzzed about the first interracial game, thus promoting the fundraiser. The game was an all-star interracial night baseball game. General admission was $1.20, while box seats were $1.80, and a portion of the receipts went to the NCNW. The rally sought to pay for the cost of the SS *Harriet Tubman*. "Our FIGHTING DOLLARS have to get into the struggle...and MORE dollars than we dreamed of...for though invasion means ultimate triumph...invasion COMES HIGH." The 1944 games were the first of several fundraisers and subsequent Bethune birthday games. The NCNW donated twenty-five tickets for soldiers at Walter Reed Hospital. The tickets were purchased by a local business in support of the NCNW.

Ticket sales also helped raise money and awareness for the SS *Harriet Tubman*. The summer 1944 issue of the *Aframerican Journal* was dedicated to the liberty ship SS *Harriet Tubman* and the woman who was its namesake. Mary Terrell wrote, "The ship which we are launching today was named for a woman who rendered invaluable service both to her country and to her race...I hope and believe that this good ship *Harriet Tubman* will work as hard to liberate those who are oppressed today on account of their religion or their race, as the woman for whom it was named labored to free her race from slavery ninety years ago." Dorothy Ferebee wrote, "The christening of this ship, in honor of the heroic woman stands as a symbol of democracy in practice. The recognition of this great woman will bring faith and courage, and fortitude to millions of American people, who, through a strengthened morale, will crusade for a greater share of responsibility." The NCNW membership contributed, and Sara Spencer Washington, roll of honor honoree, personally purchased $10,000 worth of bonds in support of the effort. The total cost of the ship was $2 million. On June 3, 1944, NCNW members traveled to South Portland, Maine, where they christened the SS *Harriet Tubman*.

In August 1945, the second-annual interracial baseball game was scheduled between the Bushwicks and Grays. The NCNW wrote to newspaper circulation managers, stating:

> *We feel that this game offers* [newspapers] *an excellent opportunity. Nearly all boys like baseball and the Grays–Bushwick tilt is something extra special. Here is an interracial game that is designed to improve racial harmony and your carriers, these youngsters, are at the impressionable age when such evidence of racial cooperation will mean much to community goodwill. A special bleacher ticket has been prepared for carriers and other youth groups to sell for $0.25.*

Jeanetta Welch Brown accepting receipts from the NCNW's baseball benefit. Arabella Denniston is to the right of Jeanetta Welch Brown. *Courtesy Mary McLeod Bethune Council House, NPS.*

Art Carter, the Washington representative of the Grays, implored the NCNW to efficiently coordinate ticket sales to ensure financial success. In a July 1945 letter, he wrote, "The most important thing that I am concerned with at this time is how many and what time will the Council want to put tickets on sale, as I have to arrange with the park people to have the tickets ready and stamped by that date." NCNW appealed to the National Sports Foundation, Inc. (NSF), an organization established to eliminate juvenile delinquency through sports. Andrew F. Jackson, executive secretary, wrote his membership with an invitation to participate with NCNW.

> [Bethune] *has done more than any other single person to improve the relations between racial groups…*[NCNW is staging their] *Second Annual Interracial Baseball Game between the World Champions* [the Grays], *members of the Negro National League, and the* [Bushwicks], *leading white semi-pro team…This year* [NCNW] *is seeking the aid of business management by requesting them to appoint a representative to meet with the committee to make final plans for this event.*

Above: Mrs. Bethune is seen at the baseball game throwing out the first ball. *Courtesy Mary McLeod Bethune Council House, NPS.*

Opposite: Mrs. Bethune with Baseball Commissioner Posey at the Council House in Washington, D.C. *Courtesy Mary McLeod Bethune Council House, NPS.*

Bethune's position on the advisory committee of NSF along with Logan Circle neighbor Adam Clayton Powell, Howard's E.B. Henderson, sportswriter Sam Lacy and Grays' owner Cumberland Posey—aided her in securing investment from local businesses. Bethune sought advertisement on streetcars. She wrote E.C. Giddings of Capital Transit to allow for a special advertisement to adorn various privately owned streetcars. The company provided NCNW with one hundred spaces on its vehicles. The posters were charged to NCNW, but the signage would boost sales. She appealed to the American Red Cross and Washington's Better Business Bureau. The second benefit added a feature: a Miss Homestead Gray. A news clipping recounted the game as a gala occasion.

[Bethune] *flew up from New Orleans to throw out the first ball. Major Harriet West, the first Negro major in the WACs, made her debut as a "crowner" of champions by bestowing the title of "Miss Homestead Grays" on winsome Eleanor Howard, as the first prize winner in a contest sponsored by* [NCNW] *in connection with the sale of tickets for the game. Miss Howard also received a $100 War Bond donated to her by* [various local businesses]. *Second prize of a $25.00 War Bond, and a bouquet of flowers went to Marjorie S. Robinson. Third prize of a $25.00 War Bond was won by Eleanor Rogers. Both first and third prize winners received an autographed baseball from the entire Grays team.* [NCNW's] *Jean Clore, chairman of the committee on arrangements did a bang-up job in creating interest and securing the cooperation of a host of council members and local business men in making the game a success.*

On June 17, 1946, NCNW members met to discuss the third-annual interracial baseball game. A doubleheader was scheduled for July 10 between the Kansas City Monarchs and the Grays, with revenue generated on a percentage basis. All donations from patrons and sponsors would go directly to NCNW. Unlike earlier games, a half hour between the two games would be devoted to a program honoring Bethune. Moreover, July 10 was Bethune's actual birthday. This game was the first promoted as the Bethune Baseball Benefit. The scorecards featured Satchel Paige on the mound on one side while the interior expressed sentiments from the Negro Leagues to Bethune.

Mary McLeod Bethune whose 71st birthday is being celebrated with this benefit baseball attraction for the [NCNW]. *Mrs. Bethune is founder and president of NCNW and founder and president emeritus of Bethune-Cookman College. The* [Grays], *Monarchs, Baltimore Giants, Philadelphia Stars and other Negro National and Negro American League teams join baseball fans and citizens throughout the world in saying "Happy Birthday" to Mrs. Bethune, and gladly give their aid to help make this benefit a success.*

The game was successful in bringing together all walks of Negro life. Bethune wrote boxer Joe Louis about the benefit game, explaining that she admired his great work for the race and that her prayers were with him. She requested that he attend the July 1946 game, even though she herself

Major Harriet West pinning the badge of honor on the individual who sold the highest number of tickets to the Homestead Grays baseball game. *Courtesy Mary McLeod Bethune Council House, NPS.*

could not attend because of a commitment in San Francisco. "I wish so much, Joe[,] that it was possible for you to simply appear on the grounds. It would mean so much to us and to the whole citizenry of this area. We want you to come to Washington just for an hour or two to give your vote of confidence to the work that I have been trying to do all these years." The NCNW collected revenue to assist in maintaining its headquarters, and Bethune's desire for increased prominence of NCNW grew with each game. NCNW's prominence was not in a vacuum but used to service the larger Negro community with social programs.

In 1947, Jean Clore's memo introduced a new attraction: a game between the Grays and the Indianapolis Clowns. Clore cited the Clowns as one of the best attractions available. The Clowns' sensational player was Roscoe "Goose" Tatum. The Morning Star Lodge #40 Elks offered to provide a special musical program dedicated to the great work of Bethune. Clore mentioned that tickets needed to be purchased early because Jackie Robinson's success meant that other Negro League players might be recruited away to

Ruth Sykes, annual birthday prizewinner, and a group including a Negro League player from the Indianapolis Clowns. *Courtesy Mary McLeod Bethune Council House, NPS.*

white major league teams. "Your attendance will serve a twofold purpose—you will see three of the topnotch teams in Negro baseball in action and at the same time help the Council…We feel confident you will be watching in action many of the men who will follow in [Robinson's] footsteps as the years go by. Don't miss this opportunity to help the Council and at the same time see some good baseball." The popularity of the game attracted support from local businesses. The NCNW House committee thanked the Mayer company for donating a dinette set, which was given away as a gate prize.

The 1948 game between the Grays and Clowns received wide coverage in the black press. Through the years, the game became a popular sectional rivalry. One sportswriter noted that the entertaining gimmicks of the Clowns would not distract the twelve thousand fans seeking a Grays win.

The Clowns, aptly named, featured comedic stunts throughout their games, such as juggling balls or bats, and a pantomiming King Tut added levity between innings.

The demise of Negro League teams ensued as white major league teams handpicked black players to integrate the Major Leagues. Many of the prominent Negro League players were too old to be recruited and played as long as they could. During its popularity, the Bethune Birthday Benefit games etched in the minds of Washingtonians the importance of gathering their nickels and dimes together in support of Negro business and the various teams and activism supporting the NCNW. These games served Bethune and the NCNW well, increasing their visibility as a national organization located in Washington.

SING A SONG FULL OF HOPE:
CONCERTS FOR CIVIL AND HUMAN RIGHTS

Bethune loved music. One biographer stated that she loved to sing, and her voice was a lyrical soprano. Her favorite song, "Let Me Call You Sweetheart," was often played during private and public events in which she was being celebrated. In 1945, in celebration of Bethune's seventieth birthday, people gathered at the Howard Theater for a night of music. The Washington *Afro-American* newspaper ran an advertisement stating, "A galaxy of stage, radio and screen stars" participated, such as Paul Robeson, Washington's own operatic singer Madame Lillian Evanti and Howard's Todd Duncan. Roll of Honor recipient Helen Gahagan Douglas served as mistress of ceremony, while Eleanor Roosevelt served on the planning committee. The tickets were $1.80 for balcony and $2.40 for orchestra seating, and all proceeds went to the NCNW. Well attended, it established another fundraising possibility. Similar to baseball games, the concerts attracted lovers of the craft and afforded interracial harmony in social settings, chipping away at segregation. At age seventy, Bethune's status shifted to that of an elder, making her more desirable as rising leaders sought to mimic her success and longevity in the public eye.

In 1945, the Hall Johnson Choir opted to celebrate its twenty-fifth anniversary in a NCNW benefit concert in Washington in conjunction with the Washington Negro Civic Opera Company, an organization that provided opportunities to train young Negro music talent throughout the

Mrs. Bethune with Washington singing group the Charioleers at the Council House for her birthday party. *Courtesy Mary McLeod Bethune Council House, NPS.*

city. The company sponsored recitals for the youth. Johnson was known for his book *Run Little Chillun* and music in Broadway folk drama. In 1935, his choir appeared in a number of films, including *Cabin in the Sky*, *Lost Horizon* and *Green Pastures*. The choir, composed of twelve men and eight women, had a repertoire of Negro spirituals, ballads, blues and traditional American standards. On a chilly October 13, 1945, Johnson's choir performed in Griffith Stadium. The concert was well attended and the audience remained for the entire two-hour program in the crisp autumn air. One commentator noted that Johnson's choir rendered the "tender poignancy" of the traditional Negro music.

On November 18, 1948, Bethune wrote Carol Brice a letter thanking her for offering to donate to the NCNW a benefit concert to support human and civil rights at New York's Carnegie Hall. Bethune wrote Brice, "This is not the first time your golden voice has been raised against injustice to our people and it will not be the last, for what better purpose could a voice such as yours be used than to fight for human and civil justice through song."

In a January 31, 1949 radio show called "Harlem USA," Bethune explained the concert's venue change. The NCNW executive board felt that some public action should be taken to demonstrate that NCNW intended to take a stand for its rights. It pressed for the abolition of bigotry in all forms and viewed the bigotry of the DAR as part of a general pattern of segregation in Washington and throughout the nation. The funds raised from the concert would be used to intensify the campaign to unite Americans for human and civil rights. Bethune secured support from Eleanor Roosevelt, New York mayor William O'Dwyer, Chairman of Phelps Stokes Fund Dr. Channing H. Tobias, boxer Joe Louis, baseball player Jackie Robinson, labor leader Maida Springer and hundreds of other prominent individuals. Thus the concert was held in New York's Carnegie Hall on February 3. Channing Tobias noted that Bethune's request was amicable because she requested only that a fundraising concert be allowed an interracial audience. When she was denied this request, "friends of democracy and freedom of both races were outraged." Bethune stated:

> *NCNW is sponsoring* [the Brice] *concert* [as] *a signal for the beginning of a nation-wide protest by* [NCNW's] *Metropolitan Councils in the major cities of the* [United States]*...I am courageously calling upon all liberal minded thinkers. Regardless of race, to join us in making this concert the epoch making symbol of our determination to wipe out bias, prejudice and discrimination. Wherever they may be found.* [NCNW] *accepts, with great gratitude*[,] *this marvelous gesture of our renowned singer Carol Brice.*

The shockwaves resulted in Eleanor Roosevelt withdrawing her DAR membership in protest and in support of the NCNW. New York Commissioner of Housing J. Raymond Jones called the DAR's decision another example of stupid prejudice and discrimination. Bethune linked the protest to fulfilling President Truman's vision of civil rights. Women united for human and civil rights linked women of all races, classes and creeds. Through seeking integration and participating in protest against unconstructive elements in society, the NCNW and others desired to make civil and human rights a living expression of daily action.

The concert had numerous sponsors. NCNW-affiliated women, such as roll of honor winners Judge Jane Bolin, Charlotte Hawkins Brown, Maida Springer, Georgianna Sibley and Mabel Staupers, as well as leaders of various national organizations, supported the concert, such as Congressman Adam Clayton Powell, NAACP's Walter White, Urban League's Eugene Kinckle Jones, Brotherhood of Sleeping Car Porters A. Philip Randolph, writer Langston Hughes, actor Canada Lee and pianist Hazel Scott. Overall, the media campaign worked well to propel NCNW into larger areas of influence as the leading Negro women's organization. Unfortunately, the change of venue impacted ticket sales. Bethune thanked Lillian Scott of the New York office of the *Chicago Defender* for providing NCNW with a satellite office to organize the concert. Bethune wrote, "I know that we would not have made the progress we did had it not been for the liberal contribution and wonderful spirit you exhibited." James Hicks of the *Afro-American* newspaper reported the concert as a disappointing failure. Hicks recounted levels of criticism from some the NCNW members who felt promotions were poorly handled, while others felt Brice was too young a talent to attract desired box office sales. He mentioned the rifts within the NCNW when the venue moved from Washington to New York and the publicity angle morphed from protest to fundraiser. Liberian Ambassador King wrote Bethune, stating that his status as a representative of a foreign government precluded him from being involved on matters of civil or political rights. Thus he declined to be a sponsor. He mentioned that, had the concert been in Washington, he would have loved to hear Ms. Brice. According to the records, the concert was not as fiscally beneficial as it could have been. Nevertheless, the money raised aided the NCNW with its ever-expanding economic needs.

JIM CROW SENDS STORK TO D.C. STREET: COMMITTEE ON SIBLEY HOSPITAL

Bethune lived a life infused with faith. She did not live a private faith but one boldly proclaiming faith in God. When she lived in Washington, she affiliated with Asbury Methodist Church, a historic church frequented by well-to-do black people.

Asbury was organized in 1836 when a group of black Methodists, led by Eli Nugent, left Foundry Methodist Episcopal Church to form their own congregation. The interracial struggle within the Methodist church reached a pique in 1844 when enslavement became a political issue. The Methodist denomination split into two churches: (Methodist Episcopal) M.E. north and M.E. south. Principally, M.E. churches in Washington were northern affiliated;

however, there are several southern affiliated within the city. The black congregants in Washington started to leave as early as 1814 to form their own congregations where they could worship without restraint. Leadership within the M.E. churches, regardless of congregation, remained in white hands. It was not until 1864 that the Washington Annual Conference was founded for the black congregations within the mid-Atlantic region. Asbury's growth mirrored the history of black America in its quest for social justice. The church employed a mission-minded ministry through soup kitchens, food pantries and housing programs for the elderly and physically challenged. Moreover, its location on Eleventh Street was within walking distance of the Council House.

On May 12, 1945, when the Washington Citizens Committee on Sibley Hospital sent a letter to Paul Cromelin, Chairman of the Board of Sibley Hospital, there was no surprise who was among the undersigned: Asbury pastor Robert M. Williams, president of the Interdenominational Ministers' Alliance and chairman of the civic committee; Washington Methodist preachers; Bethune, founder of the NCNW; Jeanetta Welch Brown, executive secretary of the NCNW; Baptist pastor William Jernigan, secretary of the Fraternal Council of Negro Churches; and Dean William Stuart Nelson, of the Howard School of Religion. They wrote, "The citizens of Washington and particularly the members of our Methodist churches are greatly disturbed over what appears to be a brutal and unchristian dereliction of duty. Will you please investigate this matter and advise us what the policy of Sibley Hospital is with regard to the care and treatment of Negroes."

Black residents had consistent problems obtaining medical treatment throughout Washington. Freedmen's Hospital, operated by Howard, provided a wealth of treatment, and Gallinger (later D.C. General) provided treatment. Sibley Hospital, operated under the auspices of the Methodist church, was not among those providing fair treatment. Sibley has its roots in the 1890s, when Lucy Webb Hayes opened the National Training School for Deaconesses and Missionaries through the Women's Home Missionary Society of the Methodist Episcopal Church in Washington. The training school recognized the need for a clinical setting within a formal hospital. William J. Sibley, a member of Foundry M.E. Church, donated $10,000 toward the building in memory of his wife, Dorethea Lowndes Sibley, in 1894. By 1925, the hospital occupied the entire block of North Capitol Street at Pierce and M Streets, and it continued to grow. Many black residents avoided Sibley because of unfair treatment. Sibley did not have an official segregationist policy, but its treatment of potential black patients conformed to segregationist beliefs.

Tacit discrimination reached an insufferable level on December 22, 1944. According to reports in the black press, at 5:00 a.m., Bernice Miles and Eleanor Sollers ventured to Sibley seeking medical attention. A pregnant Bernice Miles felt unwell, and Sollers accompanied her to the hospital. Newspapers reported that Miles was an eighteen-year-old native of Saluda, South Carolina, who ran away from home to live with her friend in Washington. Sollers left Miles on the sidewalk within a block of the hospital and went to get help. She encountered a nurse, whose indifference stung. One newspaper article commented, "Living almost in the shadow of Sibley... Both were astounded when she was denied admittance when the child was expected momentarily." Sollers returned to Miles, who had delivered the baby in sub-zero weather. The nurse refused to admit Miles and suggested they call a taxi. They waited forty minutes until a vehicle arrived to take them to Gallinger. A white cab driver refused to take the women and newborn to Gallinger. Miles, the newborn and Sollers were left on the street. One account states that the newborn and Sollers were allowed to remain in the hospital while affidavits from Pearl Miles and Ruth Brown stated that no one was allowed to remain in the hospital. Regardless, the treatment of Miles resulted in a firestorm within the Methodist church. On January 20, 1945, clergymen protested at the Methodist Building regarding the treatment of Miles. That same night, they met with Asbury's official board and Pastor Williams. They passed a resolution protesting discriminatory practices of the hospital.

In February 1945, the Negro Methodist Ministers of Washington and Vicinity rallied to action. They issued an internal letter to their bishops and pastors, saying:

> We are appealing to the Bishops and Leaders of our Church to use their influence to have an investigation of the incident and explore the policies of all our Methodist Institutions in Washington. We have been greatly embarrassed in raising our "Crusade For Christ" money when our laymen understood that some of it goes to institutions like Sibley. Again we are embarrassed when our laymen compare the policies of our institutions with others... We urgently request you write the Board of Directors of Sibley a letter requesting the dismissal of the Superintendent and nurse involved.

Mrs. J.D. Bragg, president of the Women's Division of Christian Service, inquired with Dr. Karl Meister of the Methodist Board of Hospitals and

Homes about the allegations. He dismissed the allegations as hearsay rather than true facts. Meister wrote:

> *We have taken no other steps than to determine if possible whether* [Sibley] *is affiliated with the Board of Hospitals and homes or another Board of the Church…May we assure you of our sincere desire to cooperate in every way possible to bring scientific and Christian aims and ideals into being… We have no other purpose than to aid in bringing about a Christian solution in matters which may be brought to our attention…It is unfortunate that up to the present the public has learned of one side only. The Church and its constituency through you and other officials will await the presentation of the situation from a factual and Christian viewpoint.*

Sibley management stated that it had offered treatment to over three thousand black people in 1944. Moreover, management said the woman in question was not denied admission; to the contrary, Sibley did everything it could to accommodate her.

In March, the *Zion Herald*, a Methodist publication, queried if the church would rise above the pettiness of racial prejudice. Black ministers were investigating facts and forming conclusions in support of Miles. The larger question for Methodists was whether the denomination could erase the color line of division within the church and its agencies. The *Zion Herald* reported: "Unless the church is willing to erase its color line of division within itself, it can have little moral influence in asking the nations to erase their lines of division among themselves. Moreover, the church has no argument for persuading other groups to give up their prejudices and hates until it points the way by its own practice…For Methodism to become such a brotherhood, the stain of the action of [Sibley] must be removed."

Sibley's administrative committee asserted it had interviewed Miles, who disagreed with black press accounts of her story. She was not a runaway. The weather was not below zero but was twenty-five to twenty-seven degrees above. She did walk to the hospital and fell ill outside, when her companion obtained a nurse who brought blankets outside and waited with her for an ambulance to take her to Gallinger. They concluded that one journalist was the son of a disgruntled former Methodist minister. The committee's findings led Sibley officials to dismiss Miles's case as a hoax. Caleb Queen, administrator of Sibley, wrote an article in the April edition of the *Zion Herald*, saying the whole affair was "hastily done without due consideration or even casual investigation, is grossly misleading, is injustice to our church, and it aids and abets our enemies."

Also in April, Ruth Brown, a black elevator operator at Sibley, gave an affidavit. Brown stated she was working the midnight shift on December 21. She witnessed Pearl Miles attempt to gain admission while Bernice Miles was in labor outside the hospital. She was accompanied by a woman who talked to the receiving nurse, imploring her to admit Bernice Miles. Brown left and went searching for Bernice Miles, who lay on the sidewalk with a newborn naked beside her. Brown sought to bring Bernice Miles a wheelchair when the nurse instructed her to leave the wheelchair. Brown returned to Bernice Miles and offered her coat, and the nurse provided a sheet and called an ambulance. Brown closed by saying:

> *No first aid of any kind was given, nor was either an intern or doctor called; that this affiant picked the baby up, with the umbilical cord attached and put it in the ambulance, that the mother remained on the pavement until she had discharged the placenta...This affiant has often heard receiving officials refuse to admit colored persons as bed patients although they have rendered first aid, stating that they had no beds for colored patients, as a result of this incident the affiant quit her position.*

The testimony of Brown confirmed the story of Bernice Miles. Yet Sibley officials still deemed the story a hoax. Pearl Miles provided an affidavit in May 1945 in which she admitted to assisting her sister Bernice Miles, who was feeling unwell. Initially, they sought medical assistance from Gallinger; however, the discomfort was so great that she and her sister walked toward Sibley, which "was in plain view" from where the women stood. Within half a block, Bernice fell ill and her sister went to the hospital. The nurse informed her that Negro emergencies were offered first aid assistance in the basement. When she returned to her sister, she had given birth. Pearl returned to Sibley, insistent on obtaining help as "[she] begged the nurse to admit her sister and the newborn infant; the nurse refused." The nurse suggested they get a cab to Gallinger as Pearl pleaded for assistance or instruction. The nurse offered nothing. Pearl stated, "You're a nurse, and you don't know what to do?" She asked her to call an ambulance, which the nurse did. Bernice and the baby remained outside until the ambulance came within twenty minutes of the phone call.

In May, the Washington Conference adopted a resolution that stated:

Whereas, we feel that an institution thus backed by the Church should follow the teachings of Christ, and Whereas, on December 22, 1944 a young Negro had given birth to a baby on the sidewalk within a half block of Sibley, was refused emergency treatment, admission and hospitalization by this hospital solely because of her race and was forced to remain on the sidewalk with her new-born baby in sub-freezing weather for twenty minutes or more until an ambulance arrived to take her several miles away to Gallinger and Whereas, these facts have been investigated and corroborated by the Civic Committee of the Washington Methodist Ministers' Union, the DC Branch NAACP, the Citizens Committee on Sibley Hospital and the Methodist Layman's Committee on Sibley and Whereas, we maintain that the treatment accorded this young mother is inhuman, unchristian and unworthy of a Christian institution, therefore, be it resolved, that the Washington Conference of Methodist Church in Annual Session assembled as on record as protesting the discriminatory and inhumane treatment accorded this young mother and be it resolved that this Conference request a change in the policy of Sibley and that there be no discrimination in the hospitalization of patients on account of race, color or creed.

In June, Sibley's Board of Trustees replied that after full consideration at the annual meeting in May, the board "did not deem it necessary or desirable to make or issue any statement with regard to this matter which has long since been regarded as closed." Protest letters waned, and in 1950, Sibley experienced its first black birth in its nearly seventy-year history.

Bethune's affiliation with Asbury and interest in women's health probably contributed to NCNW's interest in the 1946 Wagner-Murray-Dingell Bill, which sought to extend the social security act to include medical care and hospitalization. NCNW argued that a national health plan would be truly American because it would remove the lack of equity in physical facilities. The national coverage would end discrimination on the state level. It would offer a freedom of choice for doctors, hospital mortality rates would be reduced and doctors' incomes would increase. Unfortunately, the bill did not pass, in part from the growing tide of conservatism.

BEAUTY, HEALTH AND DELTA SIGMA THETA

The overwhelming desire to improve the position and condition of black women impelled Bethune into all arenas of wholesome living. Her faith, political involvement, social consciousness and desire to help others contributed to her sense of purpose. For black women, public image was directly related to effective refutation of stereotypes, thus her love for fine clothing and maintaining a well-coifed hairstyle affirmed the fact that black women are beautiful. The media-crafted image of black women often portrayed unruly, unkempt females who exhibited childlike tendencies or voracious sexuality. As an educator, Bethune and her generation sought to teach and model the form that young women should aspire to attain. Madame C.J. Walker, the first black female millionaire, developed a hair care system, while Annie Malone developed a hair stretching device to tame the tightly coiled curls of black women's hair. According to Tiffany Gill in *Beauty Shop Politics: African American Women's Activism in the Beauty Industry*, "Walker and Malone confronted attacks to their industry based on its seeming contradictory stance to the politics of racial uplift and marked a clear departure from the previous practices of white-owned or male-owned companies that invoked language about hair straightening to sell their products and services." These businesswomen viewed beauty culture as industry and education. Walker sought out black colleges and agents who would train and teach hair care concepts while creating a source of income. One of Walker's employees, Marjorie Stewart Joyner, went beyond employment, patenting her own invention for hair curling and straightening. Joyner was ambitious and driven, but she was denied entry to a national beauticians' contest because of her race in 1932. She encountered Bethune, and her trajectory changed. Bethune inspired Joyner to pursue another avenue in her career. Their conversation resulted in Joyner traveling to Paris, France, to learn innovations in beauty culture. Bethune infused Joyner with the spirit of a beauty ambassador on behalf of black beauticians. Their relationship blossomed. Joyner and Bethune shared visions of empowered, educated and entrepreneurial black women. The two cofounded the United Beauty School Owners and Teachers Association (UBSOTA) in 1945. The first-annual meeting of the UBSOTA was at Bethune-Cookman College in 1947. Joyner was a 1948 Roll of Honor awardee. The idea of beauty for Bethune and Joyner transcended the mere physical and incorporated a wholeness of economic, social, political and aesthetic modeling as racial uplift for all black women.

The first-annual convention of United Beauty School Owners and Teachers Association. *From left to right:* Henri Anna Carroll, Lucille La Roberts Freeman, Marjorie Stewart Joyner, Maude Gadsen. Mary McLeod Bethune appears at center. *Courtesy Mary McLeod Bethune Council House, NPS.*

Gill explained, "Through Joyner's harnessing of [black women's] political power by means of strategic organizing and philanthropy, black beauty school owners and teachers entered the Cold War era secure in their position as political brokers in their respective communities."

Bethune was interested in healthcare. As a chronic asthmatic, she knew the priceless value of available and affordable healthcare. In 1946, NCNW wanted the Wagner-Murray-Dingell Bill to pass because it would provide federal legislation ensuring all citizens with access to quality care. Although the bill did not pass, Bethune and others concerned themselves with providing resources as well as advocating for better treatment. In the 1940s, many children contracted tuberculosis or suffered from poor nutrition. NCNW, Bethune and others sought to bridge the disparities in the form of studies, lobbying for legislation and contributing to their respective faith communities, which served meals to combat this poor nutrition.

Bethune's foray into the health legislation involved desegregating the Red Cross and brought Dr. Charles Drew into her life. He was an African American physician who developed ways to process and store blood plasma in "blood banks." During World War II, he led a special medical effort known as "Blood for Britain." He organized a collection method providing blood plasma for shipments with life-saving materials overseas. He also worked on another blood bank effort, this time for the American Red Cross. During his work for the Red Cross, the blood bank would be used for U.S. military servicemen. He eventually resigned from the Red Cross because it segregated the blood donated by blacks.

Bethune's NCNW was an organization of organizations pulling together the college educated with grassroots activists working on behalf of Negro women. The four leading collegiate sororities—Alpha Kappa Alpha, Delta Sigma Theta, Zeta Phi Beta and Sigma Gamma Rho—held organizational membership in the NCNW. Many of the future national presidents of the four sororities rose through the ranks of NCNW, learning and honing their leadership skills through interorganizational and intergenerational connections. The 1940s for the NCNW represented a cohesiveness, branding them a leading organization of working women seeking to provide a better today and a brighter tomorrow. Bethune was granted honorary membership in Delta Sigma Theta. In 1946, Delta president Mae Wright Downs received a letter from Bethune, celebrating the NCNW certificate of membership for Delta as a symbol of "common unity of purpose and action." Every affiliate organization submitted reports to the NCNW of its activities on the group's behalf. The reports from Delta provide a glimpse into the parallel nature of the NCNW and Delta in select service projects. In the early 1940s, Delta maintained two field library services. It solicited books by and about Negro people, thus its launching the NCNW library drive with a donation of fifty books supported the larger agenda of literacy. In support of the Council House, Delta launched a $100,000 drive at the twentieth national convention. Individuals contributed sums of $100, while others

Opposite, top: Mrs. Bethune and NCNW members attending a health conference at the Council House. Dr. Charles Drew is in this group, standing to the far right. *Courtesy Mary McLeod Bethune Council House, NPS.*

Opposite, bottom: Mrs. Bethune and sorority members. *From left to right:* Treida Witherspoon, Juanita S. Martin, Mary McLeod Bethune, Bessie Garvin and Edwina Mitchell. *Courtesy Mary McLeod Bethune Council House, NPS.*

Above: Officers of Delta Sigma Theta Sorority, a NCNW affiliate, at a Washington Pan-Hellenic Council event. Dorothy Height is first from left. *Courtesy Mary McLeod Bethune Council House, NPS.*

Opposite, top: Mrs. Bethune, Mary Church Terrell and women in parlor. *Courtesy Mary McLeod Bethune Council House, NPS.*

Opposite, bottom: Members of Delta Sigma Theta attend a NCNW workshop. Second from the left is Dorothy Height, Mary McLeod Bethune is standing at the center and to her left is Mary Church Terrell. *Courtesy Mary McLeod Bethune Council House, NPS.*

organized within their chapters. In 1949, Delta queried chapters about their membership in the NCNW as individuals. "What is the evidence of your cooperation in the local Metropolitan Council if one is in your vicinity?" In the NCNW affiliate report, the national president implored membership to make the NCNW program a reality in every community. "With the heads of other National organizations the president of DST met in Washington to discuss ways and means of increasing our participation as national organizations in the NCNW. This was an inspiring occasion and the fruits of those efforts have not been grown fully. We have, however, a new sense of direction and responsibility." A handwritten note on the report observed:

As an honorary member of DST—Mrs. Bethune our beloved Founder President of the NCNW—gave to us the symbol of the torch of wisdom. As we pay tribute to her in these days it is our hope and prayer that not only in building a stronger but in sharing in the development of a greater NCNW we shall have the strength and the courage to hold high that torch and work unitedly for a better world in which to live. Dorothy I. Height, President.

Dorothy Height was personally invited by Bethune to join NCNW in the late 1930s and rose through the ranks, becoming the longest-serving NCNW president, from 1957 to 1998. Height was fully committed to the vision of Bethune and sought to connect every generation of young black women to the missionary purpose of a well-lived life, paying forward benefits and opportunities to ensure a viable future for all.

Bethune engaged young women and social issues passionately. She used her life as a yardstick for younger women to see the progress of the race. She inspired them to live selfless lives dedicated to greater service, ensuring greater progress for the race and humankind. While living in Washington, she experienced the sting of discrimination and rose above it in protest through the press or a signed petition. Her hearty living began to take a toll on her body. Nearing eighty years of age and suffering from bouts of asthma, Bethune realized her dream through the house and the young women rising into leadership throughout the NCNW, Washington and the world—a fitting harvest after over fifty years of sowing seeds along the eastern seaboard.

CHAPTER 5

Stepping Aside

Bethune Bids Adieu

In July 1953, Bethune described the sundown of her life as beautiful for the *Chicago Defender*: "When the long day of activity is over and the cloak of darkness stills the busy day it is good to sit and reflect...My dream child, the NCNW[,] looms clearly before me in these moments of reflection. These women united shoulder to shoulder have accepted grave responsibilities in the affairs of the world and are counted among the women of the world who are doing things." Her transition from Washington to Daytona was peaceful. She continued to write her column in the *Chicago Defender* as well as keep a full calendar. In April 1949, NBC's *This is Your Life* program featured Bethune. The tribute was sponsored by Phillip Morris Company, and Ralph Edwards served as the master of ceremonies. Friends and associates of Bethune traveled to Los Angeles to surprise her on the program. *Women United* reported:

> In a half-hour program on Tuesday evening March 15, the founder and president emeritus of Bethune-Cookman College was heard over a coast to coast network. Included guests were Mrs. Gertrude Jackson, one of the first five pupils in Mrs. Bethune's school; Mrs. Arabella Denniston graduate of Bethune-Cookman College, secretary to [Bethune for fifteen years]; Mrs. Lucy Miller Mitchell, of Boston, Mass, a pupil of Mrs. Bethune's school; Mrs. Cecelia C. Smith of Washington, D.C., a classmate of Mrs. Bethune; Leroy Bazzell, a Florida friend who as a little boy took care of Albert [her son]; Albert McLeod Bethune Jr. appeared on the program.

Ralph Edwards and Mrs. Bethune at the taping of *This Is Your Life. From left to right:* Arabella Denniston, Albert Bethune, Cecillia Smith, Leroy Bazell, Mrs. Sadie Franklin, Charlotte Ford Clark and Mrs. Lucy Mitchell. *Courtesy Mary McLeod Bethune Council House, NPS.*

Debuting on radio in 1948, *This Is Your Life* was a pioneering reality show on television. Creator-producer-host Ralph Edwards formulated the idea for *This Is Your Life* while working on another show, *Truth or Consequences.* He was tasked by the U.S. Army to produce something for soldiers in the Birmingham General Hospital rehabilitation facility in Van Nuys, California. Edwards selected a "particularly despondent young soldier" and birthed the idea of presenting his story on air in order to contextualize his whole life, thereby reducing the disastrous reality of his present condition. Edwards hoped that the solider would view his life through the happier times of the past and become inspired with hope for the future. The positive feedback resulted in the formulation of *This Is Your Life.* His format surprised each guest with a narrator telling their story. He weaved in voices from their past, hoping to jog their memories. Ultimately, the featured guest contributed to their community through impacting people's lives. Edwards believed that stars and "heroic unknowns" were equally worthy of recognition.

NCNW issued a press release in autumn 1949. "[Mrs.] Bethune was a dreamer who dreamed and brought them to human reality. She was a doer who did great deeds. She was a special force generating a power that affected thousands of people who felt the radiation of her spirit." They praised her for being a "dynamic leader" whose programs included political action, federal government involvement and the archives of Negro women pioneers. The archives were developed because Bethune inspired women "eager and willing to follow wherever she might lead." After fourteen years as president, she retired. "She left her mark on the times in which she lived. It is for the women who succeed her—her beautiful daughters to carry on." Simultaneously, Bethune cleared up apprehensions regarding her retirement. She remained involved with the NCNW but no longer at the helm of the organization.

In *Women United*, she penned an article titled "Stepping Aside at Seventy Four: A Message from Mary McLeod Bethune," which stated:

> *Women United goes to press as I make ready to turn over the president's desk at our national headquarters in Washington, to younger, stronger, surer hands, and I find, constantly passing through my mind, the faces of the women who have helped to make the foundation-laying of the NCNW, during the past fifteen years, a work of joy. I want to pay tribute to them! There are so many of these women, old and young, fine, strong, alert women, clear-headed far-seeing leaders in so many fields. How much they have meant to me! There was no idea so big they could not grasp and develop it. No task so humble that they scorned it. How they came around me and worked early and late, on problems which affected their individual lives, the lives of all women, they sought and found ways to integrate women into jobs; they joined forces to help push through legislation designed to lighten the burden of women and children; and in the far flung areas, trained and encouraged women to use the franchise to their advantage. These women worked at makeshift desks in the living room of my little apartment on Ninth Street, where my tired secretary would fall asleep, after the last volunteer had left with the dawn. And all this at the end of a hard day's work on important full-time jobs! I can never forget the friends of those early days, in the life of our beloved organization.*

Bethune viewed all NCNW members as her daughters. She believed that the NCNW was their organization—not simply her dream but rather a manifestation for all women. Bethune believed that the initial intention of the NCNW was a cry to be heard, remarking, "It was a dream of being able to say, women united for progress, without regard to race, creed, color or political affiliation."

The House held a place in her heart. Bethune recalled the early investments of members and affiliate organizations. In *Women United*, she wrote:

> *The soft velvet rug that carpets the staircase that leads to the office of the president, has felt the tread of many feet of those in need; and tired feet, like my own, these days. I walked through our headquarters, beautifully furnished by friends who caught our vision, free from debt! I walk through the lovely reception room where the great crystal chandelier reflects the colors of the international flags massed behind it—the flags of the world! I go into the paneled library with its conference table, around which so many great minds have met to work at the problems of the past years. I feel a sense of peace.*

Bethune continued her reflection on the presence the Washington headquarters provided NCNW.

> *Our headquarters is symbolic of the direction of their going, and of the quality of their leadership in the world of today and tomorrow. I have no fear for the future of women. I was sixty years old when this dream first took shape, on December 5, 1935. Now, at seventy-four, with the minds and hearts of thousands of women united to the task, I step aside and I can rest awhile! May God bless all the women who have united with me in this effort, wherever they may be. They have brains! May they have the moral power and grant that He give them the spirit to carry on, to bulwark gains already made, to blaze new trails. In Washington or wherever I am, my door and my heart will be open to all, to serve in the work of the world, in whatever way I can within the limits of my strength. God bless them all!*

NCNW fêted Bethune in grand style. There were numerous parties sending her into semi-retirement in style. The NCNW leadership crafted a resolution in celebration of her stepping down as national president. The tender feelings and admiration for Bethune is evident in the lines of good-cheer, gratitude and inspiration.

> *It is with profound sorrow to us that the night of November 18, 1949 marks the conclusion of the fourteen years of uninterrupted service of the Founder-President, Mary McLeod Bethune*

Seldom in the history of any organization does the fount of inspiration, of fortitude, of ideals, of spiritual and organizational unity, continue unabated, but with increasing strength and wisdom as has been shown by our Founder-President for a decade and a half.

With unparalleled tenacity, she founded the Council and held together, sometimes almost alone, but for the sheer force of the passion of her vision, thousands of Negro women who never before in their history had been able to achieve such unity. She gave her followers the twin qualities of PATIENCE and DETERMINATION.

She opened doors of opportunity to women of every race and color, and she projected Negro women to the highest levels of public service on a national and international level. She was responsible for the elevation of the status of Negro women as international citizens of the world.

The judgments of history must surely confirm the world estimation of her contribution to humanity.

The NCNW will enshrine the memory of her deeds and her words upon the hearts and minds and upon the records of the Council perpetuity.

A testimonial dinner for six hundred people filled the Interior Department's dining room. Resplendent in a black velvet dress with rhinestone trim and wearing a huge orchid corsage, Bethune witnessed the outpouring of affection these people had for her. The international community celebrated her retirement in conjunction with a constellation of friends and colleagues, including John Sengstacke, newspaper publisher; Benjamin Mays, president of Morehouse; and Aubrey Williams and Frank Horne from her NYA days. Sengstacke called Bethune a civil rights leader who fought for equality. Bethune passed the mantle of leadership she had worn with dignity for over ten years.

Dr. Ferebee served as the NCNW president from 1949 to 1952. "By supporting the United Nations' policies on human rights and peace, and through more focused programmatic thrusts aimed at eliminating both the segregation of and discrimination against blacks and women in health care, education, housing and the armed forces, [she] succeeded in maintaining the established NCNW program of advocacy."

Dr. Ferebee did not attempt to replace Bethune. She did expand Bethune's vision into the 1950s. The desire of the NCNW membership under Ferebee's leadership was a coming of age that built on the foundation established by Bethune. Dr. Margaret Just Butcher reflected, "The 16th annual convention emphasized ways to carry cosmopolitan ideas and universal problems into

Above: President Harry Truman, Mrs. Bethune, Madame Pandit and Dr. Ralph Bunche, from left to right, at Mrs. Bethune's final NCNW meeting as president. All were recipients of the citation for outstanding citizenship. *Courtesy of State Archives of Florida.*

Opposite, top: Retirement dinner for Mrs. Bethune at Interior Department. Mrs. Bethune, wearing the Haitian Medal of Honor and Merit, is pictured with Vivian Carter Mason to her right, while to her left is Dorothy Ferebee and to her far right is Dorothy Height. *Courtesy Mary McLeod Bethune Council House, NPS.*

Opposite, bottom: Dinner at 1949 convention honoring Mrs. Bethune. Dorothy Ferebee is at the left of the picture. Bethune is wearing the Haitian Medal of Honor and Merit. *Courtesy Mary McLeod Bethune Council House, NPS.*

'Main Street.'" Her tenure marked a change in the NCNW meetings from annual to biennial. This measure was cost effective for the NCNW office and affiliate members.

Bethune was interviewed by Lois Taylor, who asked, "If you could start your life over again, what would you do?" Bethune remarked that she would head straight to New York and run for Congress. "That's what I'd do. And I wouldn't have to run out Adam Powell, either. There's room for more there in Congress, and it's about time." She mentioned that she would consider a stint in diplomatic service, stating that diplomatic service offered opportunities and advantages for American citizens. Taylor wrote in the *Afro-American* newspaper on November 19, 1949, "The dowager lady of

Mrs. Bethune, wearing the Haitian Medal of Honor and Merit, and Dorothy Ferebee.
Courtesy Mary McLeod Bethune Council House, NPS.

the race has already done pretty well, unofficially, as politician, diplomat and business woman. The building in which we sat was itself a tribute to her astuteness in all three directions." Bethune informed Taylor that her stepping down and leaving Washington was a voluntary choice. "I'm retiring not to go aspeel [*sic*]. But I feel that I've done with the Council and it's time now to give the younger women a chance to take over, while I stand on the sidelines." Taylor viewed Bethune's retirement with justification. She had just returned from Florida and was being summoned to a luncheon with the National Conference on Christians and Jews at the Mayflower Hotel. She was also scheduled to speak in New York later that week—all of these activities happening while Bethune and NCNW staff planned their annual convention. "Honest to goodness, Mrs. Bethune, just between you and me, you really aren't taking this retirement really seriously, are you?" Bethune smiled her signature pontifical smile.

Bethune left Washington to pursue an unentangled public life and write her memoir. The expansive life of Bethune from Reconstruction to the atomic age, from colored to Negro, provided a great blueprint for young people. Her tenacious dedication to principles of fair play, honesty and faith remained pillars of her character in the face of adversity. In an article titled "The Negro in Retrospect and Prospect," Bethune stated:

> *Without indulging in self-applause, we can very well turn for a brief moment at this point in our march forward and view, with a feeling of so-far-so-good, the gains we have made and held. As mature people we shall waste no time in over-admiration. Long stretches of the road to the full life we shall achieve still lie ahead. But we are traveling with our eyes open and our wits about us, and in traversing the unseen stretches ahead we shall have the benefit of techniques developed and proved in conquering the rough terrain behind. As the Negro moves out in his newly-recognized capacity as a power to be reckoned with, it will be well to remember that not only courage but caution has a place in progress…My kind of caution would call for acceptance of the responsibility of being informed; for strengthening of moral character.*

Bethune lived her life in line with principals of piety and moral character. She attempted to provide opportunities for Negro women and girls in education and social justice. Innately gifted as a leader, she pushed herself to locate resources to provide for rising generations. A year before her departure as NCNW president, the younger generation of NCNW wrote: "It was with a mingled feeling of surprise and elation that we learned of our privilege of visiting the White House with you this coming Tuesday. How can we thank you enough! We fear words cannot express fully our sincere appreciation of your kindness and thoughtfulness. 'A kind heart is a fountain of gladness, making everything in its vicinity freshen into smiles.'"

In Washington, Bethune left mingled feelings of surprise and elation for its black residents. Her stature and sincerity touched diplomats, ambassadors, university presidents, foreign citizens, military servicemen, students, teachers and blue-collar and government workers. She exuded the confidence and articulate voice of the race. Her ebony face framed in gray hair allowed her visual accessibility in looking personally familiar while simultaneously international known.

In conclusion, Bethune's residency in Washington ushered in the modern civil rights movement. Every blow to the monster of segregation weakened it, allowing the events of 1963 to slay the hydra-headed beast. Bethune's entire public life was dedicated to reconstructing the image of black womanhood. Her childhood desire to learn, her school, her organizational affiliations and the organizations she founded sought to place black womanhood into the narrative of human history as daughters of God and sisters of humanity. Black women were maligned, abused and misrepresented in the media. Poverty and neglect further punished them for being both black and female. Bethune did not allow those external realities to cripple her momentum, however. She embraced John 3:16, which said, "For God so loved the world that He gave his only begotten son that whosoever believed in Him will not die but have everlastingly life." Bethune understood love and included herself among the "whosoever" the Bible referenced. Being in Washington centralized her activities benefiting the college, the students, the clubs and the women she fought to safeguard against ignorance, racism and economic exploitation. Selecting property in Logan Circle was strategic to becoming a neo-native Washingtonian and entertaining scores of domestic and foreign-born personalities.

It has been my hope to present this sliver of Bethune's life in detail to demonstrate the impact she had in Washington. From protesting the discriminatory policy of People's Drugstore to signing a petition against Sibley Hospital, Bethune embraced the local struggle for civil rights. Concurrently, she grew the NCNW into the leading voice of organized Negro womanhood through the Roll of Honor receptions, as well as Hold Your Job and We Serve America programs. Meeting the needs of people, advocating for fair treatment and monitoring government programs positioned the NCNW and Bethune in a unique place of strength through collaboration with other groups. In Washington's Logan Circle neighborhood, Bethune and the NCNW brought a level of activism and voice for black women. The House remained the NCNW headquarters until 1966 when a fire in the basement caused extensive damage. The NCNW had to vacate the building and take up temporary offices at 1110 Vermont Avenue, Northwest. In 1972, Logan Circle was designated a historic district. In 1982, Congress passed legislation allowing the Department of the Interior to accept 1318 Vermont Avenue and its carriage house as part of the National Park Service system. In 1994, NPS renamed the property the Mary McLeod Bethune Council House National Historic Site. The Council House is a tourist destination as well as the home of the National Archives for Black Women's History. Bethune's memorial continues to breathe life into new generations, inspiring them to pursue education and engage in activism to safeguard democracy for themselves, the less fortunate and the unborn.

APPENDIX

Bethune's Washington Timeline

1936-1949

The dates are from *Mary McLeod Bethune and the National Council of Negro Women Pursuing a True and Unfettered Democracy*, by Elaine Smith.

JUNE 24, 1936: Bethune assumed full-time government employment as specialist on Negro Affairs in the NYA. She lived at 1340 G Street, Northwest.

JULY 25, 1936: NCNW incorporated in Washington.

AUGUST 7, 1936: Bethune convened a meeting with seven government employees at 316 T Street, Northwest, which resulted in the formation of the Federal Council on Negro Affairs, commonly called the Black Cabinet.

OCTOBER 27, 1936: Bethune was elected president of ASALH.

APRIL 9, 1939: Bethune and seventy-five thousand others attend Marian Anderson's Easter concert at the Lincoln Memorial in Washington.

APRIL 1940: Inaugural issue of the *Aframerican Women's Journal,* the NCNW quarterly publication, appeared with Sue Bailey Thurman serving as editor.

OCTOBER 1940: NCNW moved its annual meeting from New York to Washington for the first time.

APRIL 1943: NCNW hired Jeanetta Welch Brown as its first full-time salaried executive secretary.

JUNE 1943: Inaugural issue of *Telefact*, the NCNW monthly newsletter, appeared, and NCNW held its first Wartime Employment Clinic.

JULY 4–10, 1943: NCNW held We Serve America Week to demonstrate the contributions of black women to the war effort.

SEPTEMBER 12–18, 1943: NCNW participated in Hold Your Job Week, an event observed in select black communities.

JANUARY 24, 1944: Bethune officially left government when the NYA office liquidated.

FEBRUARY 11, 1944: NCNW initiated the Building Better Race Relations conference. Thirty national women's organizations were invited, and Eleanor Roosevelt spoke.

OCTOBER 13, 1944: NCNW initiated International Night at its annual meeting.

OCTOBER 15, 1944: NCNW dedicated its headquarters building at 1318 Vermont Avenue, Northwest.

FEBRUARY 10, 1945: NCNW initiated a reception at headquarters with the Roll of Honor. The Roll of Honor celebrated the accomplishments of outstanding women.

APRIL 13, 1945: Bethune eulogized President Roosevelt during a national radio tribute.

JULY 10, 1945: NCNW held a Seventieth Bethune Birthday fundraiser at the Howard Theater.

OCTOBER 27, 1945: Marjorie Stewart Joyner organized the National Association of Beauty School Owners and Teachers at NCNW headquarters to serve as a clearinghouse for beauty culture schools. Bethune served as a national sponsor.

JULY 27–AUGUST 2, 1946: Bethune attended the Golden Jubilee biennial meeting of NACW.

FEBRUARY 15, 1948: NCNW hosted a formal diplomatic reception at its headquarters in honor of Haitian Ambassador Joseph D. Charles and Liberian Minister and Mrs. C.B.D. King. Representatives from other countries were in attendance among the five hundred guests.

FEBRUARY 21, 1949: Bethune received an honorary doctor of humanities degree from Rollins College in Winter Park, Florida. She was the first black person awarded a degree from Rollins.

MARCH 15, 1949: Bethune was featured on *This is Your Life*, a national television show originating in Los Angeles, California.

APRIL 1949: Bethune was photographed against the backdrop of the nation's capital, filling the cover of *Ebony* magazine, which carried her article titled "My Secret Talks with FDR."

JULY 12–22, 1949: Bethune visited the Republic of Haiti as a guest of its government and received the Order of Honor and Merit, the country's highest award. Haiti had never before bestowed this honor on a woman.

NOVEMBER 13, 1949: President Harry Truman was the guest speaker for NCNW's International Night. NCNW presented outstanding citizenship awards to United Nations Director of Trusteeship Ralph Bunche; the first woman ambassador to the United States, Vijaya Pandit of India; veteran organizational and civil rights activist Mary Church Terrell; first black circuit Judge William H. Hastie, of the Third US Circuit Court of Appeals; and twelve others.

NOVEMBER 18, 1949: NCNW hosted a gala dinner honoring Bethune on her retirement from the NCNW presidency.

Works Cited

NABWH is an abbreviation of the National Archives for Black Women's History, found at the Mary McLeod Bethune Council House, Washington, D.C.

PREFACE/INTRODUCTION

Bethune, Mary McLeod. "Takes Inventory of Friends and Foes in the Fight for Civil Rights." *Chicago Defender* National Edition June 11, 1949.

Dr. Mary McLeod Bethune interview on WINX. NABWH 001_S05_B05_F087.

"Growing Up in Washington II: Great Depression and World War II." Loretta Carter Hanes interview. Historical Society of Washington.

Johnson, Georgia Douglas. *Mary McLeod Bethune*. NABWH001_S05_B05_F092.

Open letter from Bethune to NACW. Mary Church Terrell papers, box 102-1, folder 22, Manuscript Division Moorland Spingarn Research Center, Howard University, Washington, D.C.

CHAPTER 1

Cook, Blanche Wiesen. "Woman of the Century." *Women's Review of Books* 27, nos. 10–11 (July 2000).

Holt, Rackham. *Mary McLeod Bethune: A Biography*. Garden City, NY: Doubleday & Company, Inc., 1964.

CHAPTER 2

Bethune, Mary McLeod. Interview. Monday, June 17, 1946. Transcript at NABWH 001_S05_B04_F063.

Hanson, Joyce A. *Mary McLeod Bethune & Black Women's Political Activism.* Columbia: University of Missouri, 2003.

Height, Dorothy I. *Open Wide the Gates of Freedom.* Washington D.C.: Public Affairs, 2003.

Kerr, Audrey Elisa. *The Paper Bag Principle: Class, Colorism, and Rumor and the Case of Black Washington, D.C.* Knoxville: University of Tennessee, 2006.

National Council of Negro Women archives, 1935–1949. NABWH 001_S05_B16_F263.

National Park Service. Mary McLeod Bethune Council House Historic Structure Report, 2008.

Remarks Made at the Dedicatory Services of the Building for the National Council of Negro Women, Inc. Transcript at NABWH 001_S05_B10_F182.

Smith, Elaine M. *Mary McLeod Bethune and the National Council of Negro Women: Pursuing a True and Unfettered Democracy.* Montgomery: Alabama State University, 2003.

Taylor, Rebecca Stiles. "Federated Clubs." *Chicago Defender,* October 28, 1944.

Telefacts newsletter. 1943 edition, NABWH 001_S13_B02_F30; 1944, NABWH 001_S13_B02_F31; 1946, NABWH 001_S13_B02_F32; 1947, NABWH 001_S13_B02_F33; 1948, NABWH 001_S13_B02_F34; 1949, NABWH 001_S13_B02_F35.

Thurman, Sue Bailey Thurman. "But the Greatest of These." *Aframerican Women's Journal*, Winter 1941–1942. NABWH 001_S13_B01_F09.

Women United, October 1949. NABWH 001_S13_B01_F27.

Chapter 3

Afro-American. "Mrs. Hamilton, One of God's Servants." March 8, 1958.

Atlanta Daily World. "Bethune Cites Frisco Confab Opportunity." May 1, 1945.

Bethune, Mary McLeod. "Action Letter!!" Memo to NCNW leadership. NABWH 001_S05_B11_F196.

———. "Calls Haiti Symbol of Attainable Freedom for Thousands of Blacks." *Chicago Defender*. July 23, 1949.

———. "A Challenge." WANDs newsletter. NABWH 001_S18_B08_F0097.

———. "Constructive Action Haiti Depends on Unity Among People." *Chicago Defender*. June 3, 1950.

———. "Haiti and Liberian Diplomats Honored." *Chicago Defender*, February 28, 1948.

———. "Job Security and Negro Women." *Congress Vue* 2, no. 2 (May 1944).

———. "Two Young Guests Give Insight of Woman's New Status in India." *Chicago Defender*, September 24, 1949.

Black, Allida M. *Casting Her Own Shadow: Eleanor Roosevelt and the Shaping of Postwar Liberalism*. New York: Columbia University Press, 1997.

Brown, Lieutenant General Lovonia H. "An Appeal." WANDs brochure. NABWH 001_S18_B08_F0097.

Brown, Lovonia. Letter to Bethune, January 26, 1943. NABWH 001_S18_B08_F0097.

"Building Better Race Relations." *Aframerican Women's Journal*, Summer 1944. NABWH 001_S13_B01_F14.

Criteria for selecting women to be named on "Honor Roll." NABWH 001_S05_B16_F267.

"Employment of Women" radio transcript. NABWH 001_S05_B11_F195.

Higgs, Mame Mason. Letter to Hilda Orr Fortune. January 18, 1946. NABWH 001_S05_B16_F267.

Honor Roll program. NABWH 001_S05_B16_F264.

Kittrell, Flemmie. "Consultation on Home Economics." Flemmie Kittrell papers, box 104-12, folder 27. Moorland Spingarn Research Center, Howard University, Washington, D.C.

"A People's Section for the United Nations." *Aframerican Women's Journal* (Summer/Fall 1947): 14.

Richards, Yvette. *Maida Springer: Pan Africanist & International Labor Leader*. Pittsburgh: University of Pittsburgh Press, 2000.

Spragg, Venice T. "Women of Year Honored by Council Reception." *Chicago Defender*, February 24, 1945.

Taylor, Rebecca Stiles. "National Council of Negro Women Observers We Serve America Week." *Chicago Defender*, June 26, 1943.

Wilson, Francille Rusan. "Becoming 'Woman of the Year': Sadie T.M. Alexander." *Black Women Gender and Families* 2, no. 2 (Fall 2008).

Chapter 4

Affidavit of Miss Pearl Miles. NABWH 001_S05_B15_F257.

Affidavit of Mrs. Ruth Brown. Sibley Memorial Hospital Washington, D.C. 1945-1962 1974-009 (Health and Welfare) Drew University Archives.

Afro-American. "Jim Crow Sends Stork to D.C. Street." January 6, 1945.

Bethune, Mary McLeod. Interview on "Harlem USA" radio show, January 31, 1949. NABWH 001_S05_B05_F102.

———. Letter to Carol Brice. NABWH 001_S05_B05_F097.

———. Letter to Joe Louis. NABWH 001_S05_B05_F087.

Carter, Art. Letter to Jeanette W. Brown. NABWH 001_S05_B05_F085.

Clore, Jean. Bethune Birthday Celebration memo. NABWH 001_S05_B05_F085.

Davidson, Eugene. "Home Runs and Brotherly Love." Eugene Davidson papers, box 91-1 folder 6. Manuscript Division Moorland Spingarn Research Center, Howard University, Washington, D.C.

Gill, Tiffany. *Beauty Shop Politics: African American Women's Activism in the Beauty Industry.* Chicago: University of Illinois Press, 2010.

Jackson, Andrew F. "Improving Employee-Management Relationship Through Interracial Cooperation." NABWH 001_S05_B05_F085.

Meister, Karl. Letter to Mrs. J.D. Braggs. February 20, 1945 2082-4-1:04 Sibley Memorial Hospital Washington, DC 1945-1962 1974-009 (Health and Welfare) Drew University Archives.

NCNW. "NCNW is Sponsoring a Big War Bond Rally." NABWH 001_
S05_B05_F085.

NCNW. "To Circulation Manager." NABWH 001_S05_B05_F085

Negro Methodist Ministers of Washington and Vicinity, February 12, 1945,
2082-4-1:04 Sibley Memorial Hospital Washington, DC 1945-1962
1974-009 (Health and Welfare) Drew University Archives.

Official score card from Bethune Baseball Benefit. NABWH 001_S05_B05_F085.

Sewall, Joe. "Sporting Around." Art Carter papers, box 170-19, folder 19.
Manuscript Division Moorland Spingarn Research Center, Howard
University. Washington, D.C.

Report of the Delta Sigma Theta Sorority. November 16, 1949. NABWH
001_S18_B02_F027.

"Resolution of the Washington Conference." May 17, 1945. NABWH 001_
S05_B15_F257.

Washington Citizens Committee on Sibley Hospital. Letter to Paul Cromelin.
NABWH 001_S05_B15_F257.

"Woman's Council Has Ball Game." NABWH 001_S05_B05_F085.

Zion Herald. March 28, 1945 clipping 2082-4-1:04 Sibley Memorial Hospital
Washington, D.C. 1945–1962 1974-009 (Health and Welfare) Drew
University Archives.

———. April 25, 1945 clipping 2082-4-1:04 Sibley Memorial Hospital
Washington, D.C. 1945–1962 1974-009 (Health and Welfare) Drew
University Archives.

CHAPTER 5

Bethune, Mary McLeod. "Mrs. Mary Bethune Describes the Sundown of
Her Life as Beautiful." *Chicago Defender.* July 18, 1953.

————. "The Negro in Retrospect and Prospect." *Journal of Negro History* 35, no. 1 (January 1950): 17.

————. "Stepping Aside at Seventy Four: A Message from Mary McLeod Bethune." *Women United*, October 1949. NABWH 001_S13_B01_F27.

Collier-Thomas, Bettye. *N.C.N.W.: 1935–1980*. Washington, D.C.: National Council of Negro Women, 1981.

Letter to Bethune from the younger generation of the council. NABWH 001_S17_B29_F474.

NCNW. Press release. Autumn 1949. NABWH 001S05_B05_F092.

————. "Resolution for Mary McLeod Bethune." *Women United*, January 1950. NABWH 001_S13_B01_F28.

Taylor, Lois. "Would Head for Congress, Says Retiring National Council Head." *Afro American*. November 19, 1949.

"This is Your Life…Mary McLeod Bethune." *Women United*, April 1949.

Index

About the Author

D r. Ida E. Jones is a native of Cambridge, Massachusetts, and is the assistant curator of manuscripts at the Moorland-Spingarn Research Center. Her areas of interest revolve around African American Christianity, women and archives. She appeared on C-SPAN as the moderator for a discussion on the ninetieth anniversary of women's suffrage. She is a consummate public scholar who seeks to inform people about the gravity that history and historical studies have on everyday life. She holds a BA in journalism and PhD in American  history from Howard University. Currently, she is the national director of the Association of Black Women Historians.